FAMINE
GALWAY'S
DARKEST YEARS

D1353880

FAMINE
GALWAY'S
DARKEST YEARS

William Henry

MERCIER PRESS
IRISH PUBLISHER – IRISH STORY

MERCIER PRESS

Cork

www.mercierpress.ie

© Foreword: Bernard O'Hara, 2011

© Text: William Henry, 2011

978 1 85635 753 1

10 9 8 7 6 5 4 3 2 1

A CIP record for this title is available from the British Library

Printed and bound in the EU.

BY THE SAME AUTHOR

*The Shimmering Waste: The Life and Times of
Robert O'Hara Burke*

St Clerans: The Tale of a Manor House

The Lynch Family of Galway

Role of Honour: The Mayors of Galway City, 1485–2001

Mervue, 1955–2003

The Galway Arms Golfing Society

Fields of Slaughter: The Battle of Knockdoe, 1504

Supreme Sacrifice: The Story of Éamonn Ceannt, 1881–1916

Galway and the Great War

Forgotten Heroes: Galway Soldiers of the Great War

Galway's Great War Memorial Book, 1914–18

Tír na nÓg: A New Adventure

Coffin Ship: The Wreck of the Brig St. John

IN MEMORY
OF ALL WHO LOST THEIR LIVES
IN THE GREAT FAMINE OF 1845–50

The Famine

Striding nearer every day,
like a wolf in search of prey
comes the famine on his way.

Through the dark hill, through the glen,
Over lawn, and moor, and fen,
Questing out the homes of men.

And a Voice cries overhead,
Rend your hair! The hot tears shed!
You shall starve for want of bread.

Though your wail be long and loud,
Hope for nothing from the proud,
Dig the grave, and weave the shroud.

Seek a place where ye may die,
Clench the teeth and check the sigh,
Hope! But only hope on High.

Heremon

Contents

Acknowledgements

Thanks to the following people: my wife Noreen, sons Patrick and David and daughter Lisa. Grateful appreciation to the National Library of Ireland, Dublin; the staff of Clare County Library and Clare Local Studies Project; the staff of the James Hardiman Library, National University of Ireland, Galway – Marie Boran, Geraldine Curtain, Professor Steven Ellis, Michael Faherty, Liam Frehan, Anne Mitchell and Michael O'Connor; County Galway Library, Island House, Maureen Moran and Mary Kavanagh. To all in the media – Galway Bay FM, Raidió na Gaeltachta, the *Connacht Tribune*, the *Tuam Herald*, the *Galway Advertiser*, the *Galway Independent* – including those who gave excellent publicity to this project: Brendan Carroll, Dave Hickey, Des Kelly, Dickie Byrne, Éamonn Howley, James Mitchell, Jim Carney, Jimmy Norman, Joe O'Shaughnessy, Keith Finnegan, Laura Walsh, Lisa Henry, Mark Kennedy, Máirtín Tom Sheáinin, Mary Conroy, Tom Kenny, Tom Gilmore, Peadar O'Dowd, Ronnie O'Gorman and Walter Raftery. To the staff of the Skibbereen Heritage Centre.

Special thanks also to James Casserly, Tim Collins, Anne Maria Furey, Kieran Hoare, Diarmuid Ó Cearbhaill, Pamela O'Hanlon, Bill and Alice Scanlan, Marita Silke and Mary Waller for proofreading my work and making many valuable suggestions. I am again deeply indebted to a very special friend,

Jacqueline O'Brien, who has, as always, given so generously of her time, researching and proofreading, for her expert advice, encouragement and support throughout this project.

FOREWORD

There were several regional famines in Ireland over the centuries, culminating in the last and best-remembered one, the Great Famine, from 1845 to 1850. The population of the country had increased from 3 million in 1800 to over 8 million in 1841. By the early 1840s this huge growth in population was putting increasing pressure on the fragile subsistence agrarian economy of the period as land was subdivided into smaller and smaller plots. Destitution became common, evictions increased, and emigration was taking place on a large scale.

Most of the impoverished population depended on the potato as their staple food product because of its nutritional value and high productivity (a small plot could produce enough potatoes to feed a family for a year). Disaster struck in August 1845, when a fungal disease, generally called potato blight and later identified as *Phytophthora infestans*, started to destroy the potato crop. The green stalks of potato ridges were soon producing a terrible stench. About a third of the national potato crop was destroyed that year, and an almost complete failure the following year resulted in a catastrophe. By 'Black Forty-Seven' people were dying in their thousands from starvation-related diseases, with contemporary reports recording dead bodies everywhere. By the time the Great Famine was over, it was estimated that 1 million people had died and that a further million had gone into exile, with the cottier and agricultural labouring classes, in particular, decimated.

As Ireland was part of the British Empire, and Britain was the wealthiest nation in the world, the question is always asked if its government could and should have done more to avert or mitigate the Great Famine. This issue generated considerable anti-British sentiment in Ireland and among the Irish diaspora, as well as arousing resentment against the landlord system in Ireland. The harrowing experience of the Great Famine period left a legacy of bitter memories that shaped the later history of the country. On 31 May 1997 the British Prime Minister, Tony Blair, apologised for the role of the then British government during the Great Famine in Ireland.

Many fine books have been written about the Great Irish Famine, especially in recent years, and William Henry's *Famine: Galway's Darkest Years* is a most welcome addition to that literature. He already has an impressive list of publications, especially relating to aspects of the history of Galway. This book is an absorbing, harrowing and concise history of the dreadful years of the Great Famine and its aftermath. Drawing on a variety of printed and electronic sources, especially material relating to Galway in various journals and newspapers, the author has succeeded in conveying some understanding of the suffering and misery experienced by people in those times. He explores the aetiology of the Great Famine, the arrival and development of the fungal disease, the political and economic ideologies of two British administrations, Tory and Whig, and the parsimonious measures taken to mitigate the scale of the catastrophe.

A real strength of the book is the contemporary eyewitness accounts of personal want, suffering, disease and death, as well as a society unable to respond in any effective way for a variety of reasons. Another attractive feature is the manner in which the author follows the emigrants and describes their journeys from early inhospitable receptions and prejudice to recognition and acceptance in their adopted countries. The erection of Irish famine memorials, including John Behan's *Famine Ship* at Murrisk in County Mayo and others in various cities around the world, brings welcome recognition. Finally, the author discusses the legacy of the Great Famine on subsequent developments in Irish history to 1922.

Bernard O'Hara
Registrar
Galway-Mayo Institute of Technology

Interior of a peasant's cottage.
(*The Pictorial Times*, 1846)

INTRODUCTION

One of the most tragic and appalling events in Irish history was without doubt the Great Famine that ravaged Ireland between the years 1845 and 1850. The sheer scale and horror of the devastation was terrifying. While outbreaks of famine were not uncommon in Ireland, the scale of the catastrophe that began sweeping across the country in the late summer of 1845 had never been witnessed before. It caused the deaths of over a million people, and at least another million fled the country. These figures are a conservative estimate, as the true numbers will never be known. The population of Ireland at the time of the famine was over 8 million people, the vast majority of whom were dependent on the potato, and when the crop failed the consequences were devastating. The government and authorities were warned repeatedly of the danger of the peasant population's dependence on potatoes as their source of food, but these warnings were ignored. When the blight did strike, there was no alternative food being harvested to feed the hungry peasant population.

Nevertheless, reports do indicate that there was sufficient food available in Ireland to feed its population, and that the scarcity was created by exporters. The export of grain and live-stock out of Ireland continued during the famine years, and calls for an end to this trade were ignored by traders. To make matters worse, the government did little to stop the exports. Some reports indicate that the government spent some £7 million on famine relief, which was a mere 5 per cent of its gross national profit for the period.[1] If such indifference was apparent in any famine-stricken country today there would be a public outcry and condemnation from governments across the world, but this did not happen when Ireland starved.

This book gives a brief history of the origins and effects of the Irish famine, but it is essentially the story of Galway and the Great Famine. It follows a general chronological order from the Act of Union and the background to the famine, and then moves through the famine years. It includes the uprising of 1848, the story of the famine ships and some of the horrors and disasters, particularly the loss of the brig *St. John*. It briefly introduces the reader to some of the emigrants who achieved fame and notoriety through military service, as this was initially the only profession into which the Irish were actually 'welcomed' in the USA. It also takes a brief look at the bigotry, racism and aftermath of this emigration and the remembrance and acknowledgement of Ireland's great catastrophe abroad. It is important to note just how fast some of the Irish famine refugees rose above a background of poverty in their adopted countries. The book concludes with the far-reaching effects of the famine, which is essentially a concise history of Ireland from that period to the foundation of the Irish state.

Many sources were explored during the research for this book, including the very important contemporary newspapers from 1845 to 1850 which proved an invaluable source of information. These newspapers record in graphic detail the horrors suffered by the people without the fear of political correctness, using words such as 'extermination' and 'murder'. Such reports will give the reader a good insight into the feelings of the eyewitnesses. Some may say that newspapers require a critical analysis, and this is correct; however, they are nonetheless a vital and important source of information as they portray the news as it was happening. While many other sources were explored, it is these accounts that have proved the most harrowing, and they are used and quoted because these are the experiences of the people who suffered. Rather than include all the details of one aspect of the famine in a single chapter, such as the workhouse, evictions, destitution, prison, etc., examples of these subjects can be found in each of the relevant chapters as they featured throughout all of the famine years. The book also contains personal accounts of people who suffered and died. It is important to record their names, as they represent over 2 million people who suffered similar hardship and death. A contemporary poem is also included to close each chapter. The spelling of some words in the poems may seem inaccurate, but this is how the original source recorded them. The same is true of some of the quotes.

While Galway would not spring as readily to mind as Skibbereen for suffering, it did nonetheless suffer its own horrors during the famine years. There are many parallels between what happened in Galway and Skibbereen, and examples of these are given. Skibbereen proved to be one of the worst-hit areas – not just in Cork, but in the entire country. The horrific accounts that emerged from this small area alone shocked all who witnessed or read about them; this can also be said for

Galway and the surrounding areas. Comparisons are also made between the situation in Galway and harrowing incidents that occurred in Mayo, another county that suffered greatly during the catastrophe.

Being a port town and the capital of Connacht, Galway witnessed daily an influx of human misery and the suffering of destitute people seeking 'salvation' in the dreaded workhouse. The only escape route for many people was to place themselves at the mercy of the sea and the long perilous voyage on board one of the many coffin ships that served Galway during those years. The journey to the United States and Canada was long and hazardous and proved fatal for many thousands of people in their weakened state. For those killed by disease during the voyages there was only a watery grave; all of them were consigned to the sea, sometimes without so much as a simple acknowledgement.

Irish peasants worked hard and laboured for long hours in a landlord system backed by the government, both of which failed them when their very lives depended on them most for guidance and support. Security was non-existent for most Irish tenants, and they were at the mercy of the landlord and his agents. Evictions were the order of the day for those who could not pay the excessive rents expected. In many cases, destitution and starvation were the penalty for unpaid rents for a land which had been confiscated from their forefathers. Winter or summer made no difference, nor did the sound of crying children and pleading mothers as their heartfelt pleas fell on a merciless authority. These victims were treated with indifference and sometimes even contempt. This system and government policies in the years before the famine had, in a sense, sealed the fate of the Irish people in 1845.

Starvation and disease stalked every bótharín and road of Ireland; people died along the public highways and ditches. Their humble dwellings, hovels and huts became tombs for those unable to make their way to the relief stations, soup kitchens or the workhouse. There are frightening reports of entire families starving to death in their huts with scarcely a rag to cover and protect them from bitter cold winters. As 1847 dawned the death toll was rising, bringing with it all the horrors of human suffering and misery; before the end of that year it had earned the infamous name 'Black Forty-Seven'.

Most people dreaded the workhouse not just because of its strict rules but because it was a place where disease spread easily. Fever and diseases such as dysentery, dropsy and cholera were widespread in these places, and the death toll mounted enormously during the famine years. However, as the famine progressed, they became places of refuge for the most desperate, and people besieged them, scrambling to be admitted. While much criticism has been aimed at the workhouses, it must be understood that the system was totally overwhelmed by the situation as it had not been set up to cope with the scale of the catastrophe that arrived on Ireland's doorstep in 1845. Outdoor relief, work schemes and soup kitchens were also set up throughout Ireland to try to alleviate the suffering. The soup kitchens proved successful, but they were short-lived, leaving in their wake the fear of starvation. Much of this fear was well founded, and it became a reality in a very short time. Benevolent societies sprang up to support the poverty-stricken. Many members of the clergy, both nuns and priests, as well as lay brothers did their utmost to ease the suffering, but the scale of the tragedy was far too great for them to combat it with success. Despite the misconception held by some people that priests did not die during the famine, many died of fever contracted while administering to the sick.

This book proved difficult to research, not in a physically tiring sense, but rather in an emotional sense. It is a truly poignant and heartbreaking story of a people with no security, no civil rights, no independence or voice and, in the end, no food. The following pages record the moving and harrowing story of how an enslaved people starved and died in the land of their birth having been shown little compassion.

1

PATH TO HUNGER

The Act of Union, which was introduced on 1 January 1801, was supposed to solve the problems of Ireland. This act dissolved the Irish parliament in Dublin, leaving the parliament at Westminster to legislate for both Ireland and Britain. It was described as a marriage between the two countries, and at first it seemed that Ireland had much to gain from this union. Much-needed investment and free trade between both countries was promised, and there was to be an end to discrimination by Britain against Irish industry, which had been common practice at the time. It was also believed that Catholic emancipation would follow in its wake, which would be beneficial for three-quarters of the population of Ireland. However, the harsh reality was very different, and within a short time contemporaries were describing the marriage as a 'brutal rape'. The 'free trade' enabled Britain to use Ireland as a market for surplus goods, and the promised investment did not materialise. Unemployment became widespread as Irish industry collapsed under this direct administration; Catholic emancipation was not granted until 1829 and only then after a long and desperate struggle. The repeal of the Union became the most important objective for the Irish peasantry, and in the years leading up to the Great Famine the campaigns against the so-called 'marriage' gathered momentum.[1]

Mullins hut in Skull, County Cork.
(*The Illustrated London News*, 1847)

At the head of the repeal movement stood Daniel O'Connell from County Kerry. Under his leadership, the repeal movement gained vast support amongst the Irish peasants. O'Connell was their only hope of deliverance, their great 'Liberator' as he became known. From March 1843, O'Connell began holding 'monster meetings' demanding the repeal of the Union. He chose sites with a prominent Irish historical significance for his meetings, such as the hill of Tara in County Meath where some quarter of a million people gathered to listen and support him.[2] He also held a monster meeting at Shantalla in Galway that same year, drawing massive crowds. He was met outside the old city by various organisations, and a band escorted him into Galway. His visit was welcomed by the thousands of people who came from all over the county and many parts of Connacht; they were out in force to hear him speak.[3]

Another monster meeting was planned for 8 October 1843 at Clontarf. This was another very significant location, where over 800 years earlier a great Irish victory was won over the Vikings at the Battle of Clontarf. The government were extremely worried at this stage as they recognised the powerful following that O'Connell had among the masses. Given the significance of this site, and believing that a rising would follow this gathering, the authorities banned the meeting. They had warships deployed to Dublin Bay and sent troops to occupy the approach roads to Clontarf. When O'Connell was informed of the measures now being taken by the government, he became extremely concerned. He had never before been faced with such opposition, and, fearing that a massacre might take place if he went ahead with his plans, he cancelled the meeting. He was arrested a week later and sent to prison. This experience shocked him to such a degree that when he was released a year later he was a completely changed man. He had lost his nerve while in prison, and with it the Irish people lost all hope of repeal.[4]

As constitutional methods failed to make an impact on government policies, the general population were forced into 'helpless hostility'. There was in fact a larger military presence in Ireland than in India at the time, which seems incredible given the physical comparison in size between the countries. The following statement by the Whig politician, Thomas Babington Macaulay, in February 1844, gives some idea of the animosity of some members of the government. Speaking of Ireland to the House of Commons, Macaulay said, 'How do you govern it?' He answered this question himself by saying, 'Not by love but by fear ... not by the confidence of the people but by means of armed men and entrenched camps.'[5] This type of attitude was typical of many leading politicians of the period, and, given the landlords' policies in Ireland, it was a recipe for disaster. Many visitors to Ireland at the time were appalled at the extreme human misery they witnessed among the people. One Frenchman observed that the plight of the Irish peasant was worse than that of African slaves. He said that the poorest among the 'Letts, the Estonians and the Finlanders' had a better and more comfortable lifestyle than did the Irish.[6] Hely Dutton, who carried out a statistical survey of County Galway, made the following comment with regard to both absentee and resident landlords and their attitude towards their tenants: 'What the devil do I care how they live, so long as they come to work when I want them and pay the rent.'[7]

Adding to the problems was the 'middleman system' introduced by absentee landlords to rid themselves of the responsibility of running their estates while at the same time ensuring a regular income. In many cases, these 'middlemen' were more ruthless than the landlords who employed them. The terms of lease were harsh in the extreme, and there was little security for any tenant. They were tenants 'at will', which meant that they were at the mercy of the landlord or middlemen and could be evicted at any time.[8]

Tom Sullivan of County Kerry contemplates the extent of the blight.
(*The Pictorial Times*, 1846)

Tenant housing at the time was extremely basic, consisting mainly of small thatched buildings or small one-roomed huts constructed of stone and sometimes turf. Both were very primitive, but the huts were positively dreadful places to live. These buildings had no windows so there was little daylight. There was no chimney either, just a hole in the roof to allow smoke from the fire to escape. In many cases families slept on makeshift beds of straw and a cloth covering located on a dirt floor. As can be expected from living in such improvised conditions, infant mortality was high.[9] Because of the rigid land division and landlord policies, the vast majority of the Catholic population of Ireland was forced to live on the fringes of starvation and destitution on a continual basis.[10] There was no compensation for any improvements they made to their 'holdings', which discouraged tenants from improving their actual living conditions, thus forcing them to live in squalor. Only in certain cases was compensation ever made available, but this was exceptional and only forthcoming from benevolent landlords. It seems that compensation for any work carried out was more common in Ulster. As with people in all walks of life, there were some good landlords who tried to improve living conditions for their tenants, but the brutality of others far surpassed any deeds of kindness and has left bitter memories to present times.[11]

To understand how landlords gained such absolute power over the vast majority of people in Ireland, one must look back to the introduction of the dreaded Penal Laws in 1695. These unjust laws deprived the Catholic majority of many civil rights including education, religious freedom and the ownership of the land on which they lived and worked. These laws paved the way for the rise of an ascendancy class, the majority of whom were Anglo-Irish and British families, and gave them almost limitless power over their tenants.[12] The rents were high and tenants had no protection against eviction if they could not meet the demands for payment.[13]

The saving grace for the Irish peasant throughout those years had always been the potato. It was cheap, plentiful and easily grown and was an excellent source of vitamins for the poor.[14] Once they had their crop of potatoes sown, tenants were free to 'work off' their rent or part of their rent owed to the landlord.[15] Throughout all of this hardship, hospitality and good manners among the Irish peasantry were well noted, and neighbours and indeed strangers always found a greeting upon arriving at their humble dwellings. One was welcome to sit with a family and share in whatever food was available. The pastime for most during the long winter nights was sharing stories, legends and songs and playing the fiddle. Sometimes there was a bottle of poitín available to boost up the songs, dance and stories.[16]

The system in which Ireland found itself at the turn of the nineteenth century, and the ever-increasing population, paved the way for the devastation of the famine. The population of Ireland began to increase at an extraordinary rate from 1780. Estimates for 1800 indicate a population of some 3 million people. By 1845 it had more than doubled, reaching some 8.2 million.[17] Some sources indicate that the population was even higher – over 9 million by the time of the famine. The reason for this population explosion has never been fully explained, but England and Wales also saw a rapid increase in population during this period. There was always a plentiful supply of food, provided the potato crop did not fail. Heat was provided by turf, and children were insurance against destitution in old age. However, with the increase in population, demand for land on which to grow potatoes reached massive proportions. This led to division and subdivision as parents shared their land with their children – they had little choice as the alternative meant starvation for their offspring.

This situation continued, and in a relatively short time disaster loomed. These circumstances resulted in very brutal living conditions, with a number of families, from three up to ten, occupying land that could only comfortably produce enough food for one family. This also resulted in enormously high rents which were well above the rates in England. Those forced off the land were left to live on the side of the road, and some made their way into the already overcrowded towns and cities, where they were forced to beg in order to survive.[18]

In January 1847, the following poem was published in *The Galway Mercury* under the heading 'The Starving Irish':

THE IRISH LABOURERS' *PATER NOSTRE*

Give us this day our daily bread,
Father in mercy hear our prayer,
All hope in human aid is fled,
We sink in deep despair.

Our little ones scream out in pain,
And clamour to be fed,
Father, they cry to us in vain,
Give us this day our daily bread.

O'er the gaunt infant at the breast,
The mother bows her head,
The fount is dry, in vain 'tis prest,
Give us this day our daily bread.

Our eldest born, with hollow eye,
And eager stealthy tread,
Would take the food we cannot buy,
Give us this day our daily bread.

We must not beg – he shall not steal,
Though stores before us spread,
But we will work with earnest zeal
Give us this day our daily bread.

Famine hath laid her withering hand,
Upon each little head,
O Christ! Is this a Christian land?
Give us this day our daily bread.

Thy will be done – Father receive,
Our souls when we are dead,
In Heaven we shall pine and grieve,
Or want our daily bread.[19]

2

THE BLIGHT APPEARS

The precarious situation developing in Ireland at this time is also evident from the official reports. From the foundation of the Act of Union, some 114 commissions and sixty-one committees reported on the stress in Ireland. All of them predicted disaster and stated that Ireland was on the 'verge of starvation' and also specified that the people were living in appalling conditions.[1] The situation was such that in 1843 the Devon Commission examined the Irish economic system and it reported that landlord policies were the main cause of the widespread poverty and lack of security among the people.[2] The report stated that the absolute power of the landlord over his tenants was such that they physically trembled before him, that the whole agricultural population could be evicted at the will of a landlord and that the Irish peasantry was one of the most destitute in Europe. The only food in many districts was the potato and the only beverage was water. The houses were seldom protected from the weather, and a 'bed or a blanket is a rare luxury'.[3] One member of the commission stated that the people of Ireland were the 'worst fed, worst clothed, but were the most patient people in Europe'.[4] The Devon Commission made it very clear that the stage was set for a major disaster in Ireland. This report was released in February 1845, just months before the famine struck, which seems a bit ominous.[5]

The Galway Central Hospital, formerly Galway Workhouse, 1956.
(Courtesy Fr James Mitchell)

In June 1845, frightening reports began arriving from Europe of a new blight that had been noticed in Belgium. It was not known for certain where the blight had originated, but it was believed to have come from South America some two years earlier and was perhaps carried to Europe in fertiliser consignments. The blight had an immediate effect, with thousands of people dying across France, Germany, Switzerland and the Netherlands because of huge crop failures. However, people living in these parts of Europe were not as dependent on the potato as those living in Ireland, and a severe drought in Europe the following year helped kill the blight, thus avoiding the catastrophe that struck the Irish. The blight was a type of fungus, *Phytophthora infestans*, with spores that were carried on the wind. Once the spores landed and found their way into the potato pits, they would spread again when the seed potatoes were being planted in the springtime.[6]

In September 1845, David Moore, curator of the Botanic Gardens in Dublin, stated that specimens of potatoes sent to him from Wexford and Waterford showed convincing proof of the rapid progress this alarming disease was making. At first he blamed the weather, which had been cold and damp in July and August; this led others to believe that it was dampness and not a fungus that caused the blight. Some stems looked fertile above ground, but when dug up the roots were found to be rotten and when stored away they would decompose into a putrid mass. Reports from Mayo stated that there was an 'intolerable stench' during the digging of the potato crops.[7] A number of other theories were also put forward for the crop failures. Was it static electricity caused by the latest mode of transport, the locomotive, which had just been introduced in Ireland? Was it vapours rising from volcanoes in the earth's interior? Or was it guano manure, the droppings of sea birds?[8] Regardless of the causes, the blight had arrived, and people were concerned. The following letter was published in *The Galway Mercury* in October 1845. While it gave the readers a degree of confidence that they would be protected against the failure of the potato crop if indeed there was any blight, at the same time it called for an end to the export of corn. This would indicate that the author of the letter suspected that the situation was serious. It was one of the first requests regarding the cessation of the export of corn to be made public:

We cannot more particularly allude to the rumours that have gone abroad, upon the subject of the appearance of disease among the potatoes, than to assure the public that active steps have been taken by our leading gentry, and by the inhabitants generally, to guard against any extensive failure, should such be found, on minute enquiry, to exist. No doubt there are some instances in which there can be no question as to the appearance of the rot, but on occasions of this kind, alarmists will be found to propagate rumours, and to spread dismay among the community, which will turn out to be unfounded. We will, next week, be in a condition to speak more fully on this subject. Meantime it would be well that corn of all kinds should not be exported.[9]

Although the government was warned, it simply did not react as it should have done. In fact, as the disaster was unfolding, the British Prime Minister, Sir Robert Peel, stated, 'There is such a tendency to exaggeration and inaccuracy in Irish reports that delay in acting upon them is always desirable.'[10] He also tried to introduce a Coercion Bill to ensure that law and order would not break down in the face of hostility from a hungry population; however, this Bill was not passed. He did send people to Ireland to examine the situation; in their report they overstressed the situation at the time, saying that half the potato crop had failed or was unfit for use – which was an exaggeration because there was enough to feed the people until the next harvest.[11] By December 1845, the price of potatoes had doubled; this coincided with a general increase in the overall cost of living.

Turbulent opening of a store in Cork selling Peel's Indian Corn.
(*The Illustrated London News*, 1846)

Meanwhile, the export of Irish grain to Britain continued as normal. Because the Irish market was small, it could not afford the high prices, and traders were not prepared to sacrifice any of their profits. Despite public meetings demanding an end to this trading and prominent citizens calling for exports to be stopped, food continued to leave Ireland.[12] The Irish revolutionary John Mitchel once wrote that there was enough food being exported out of Ireland to feed 18 million people and that a grain ship sailing into an Irish port was likely to meet six ships sailing out of Ireland with a similar cargo.[13] In order to stop exports, the

Corn Laws would have to be repealed, and there was massive opposition to this in Britain. The Corn Laws, as they stood, ensured that high taxes had to be paid on any foreign crops being imported into Britain, thus keeping grain prices high.

At this stage, Peel realised that to avoid starvation in Ireland corn would have to be provided from some source. Without the knowledge of his party members, he purchased £100,000 worth of Indian corn from America. While his intentions were good, this corn proved difficult to mill and even harder for people to digest. Because of this, and its colour, it became known as 'Peel's Brimstone'. While the Indian corn was unpopular at first, demand for it rose as the famine progressed. It was later replaced with imports of cornmeal rather than grain, and, when mixed with oatmeal, this was easier on the digestive system.[14]

Eventually, the growing crisis in Ireland gave Robert Peel an excuse to repeal the Corn Laws. However, their removal brought Ireland little benefit. The real problem was not so much a lack of food, as there was plenty of wheat, meat and dairy produce in the country. The problem was the exports combined with the fact that the Irish peasants did not have the money to purchase the food. There was a saying among the people at the time that 'God sent the blight, but the English made the famine', and this was true to some extent as both governments, that of Peel and, later, his successor, Lord John Russell of the Whigs, did little to help the Irish people.[15] The poem 'The Curse of the Whigs', included at the end of this chapter, clearly indicates their indifference to the suffering of the famine victims. Both *The Evening Packet* and *The Galway Vindicator* published it in 1847.

Peel also initiated a Relief Commission; its purpose was to set up food depots throughout Ireland. However, they were not allowed to sell the grain directly to the people themselves as it would affect the trader's profits; instead they sold it to local relief committees at cost price. These committees were to sell it on to the people. While the relief committees were ordered not to issue food free to the people, they did so in certain extreme cases. The financial support for the administration of the system came from the British Treasury. The Assistant Secretary to the Treasury at the time was Charles Edward Trevelyan. This was his official title, but he was in fact the permanent head of the Treasury. Although some would argue that he worked hard on relief schemes, he was against the idea of providing free famine aid. Indeed, his attitude towards the Irish people was appalling. He believed that the famine was a punishment by God on an idle, ungrateful and rebellious country. Trevelyan is immortalised in the song 'The Fields of Athenry': 'for we stole Trevelyan's corn so the young might see the morn'.

The Relief Commission decided that employment on relief works would provide peasants with a means of earning money to support themselves. This employment mainly consisted of road-works. Landlords were expected to provide some of the finance for these schemes, but this proved impossible to enforce in most cases. Those who did support the idea wanted to employ the workers on their own estates, enlarging and repairing boundary walls and in some cases building 'follies' which were of no actual benefit to anyone except to enhance a landlord's estate.[16] Some landlords also had additional works carried out. For example, at St Clerans near Craughwell, County Galway, James Hardiman

Burke created employment by having parts of the Cleran river, which ran through his land, diverted and straightened in some sections. He also added little waterfalls and ponds to embellish his estate. One of his daughters set up a soup kitchen in the old Burke castle close by.[17]

The Curse of the Whigs

It is over the upland and over the moor,
It is over the rich, it is over the poor,
It is over the valley and over the hill,
It is over seas, harbour, lough, rivers, and rill,
It is over the mansion, where Dives reside,
It is over the cabin where Lazarus hides,
O'er the rich man, who toils not, the poor man, who digs,
Is darkly impending – 'The Curse of the Whigs'.

Go forth to the fields they are bare and untilled,
Though with hunger and sickness the cabins are filled,
Though famine is sowing for next year fresh seeds,
See thousands of acres producing but weeds!
And ask ye what cause to such ruin has led,
To a present so fearful – a future so dead,
And the rich man, who toils not – the poor man, who digs,
Will answer 'The Curse – the Black Curse of the Whigs!'

Go forth through our cities, where Commerce should dwell,
And enter the warehouse, the shop, the hotel,
And try can you find any evidence there,

But of pending insolvency – hopeless despair,
Then ask why are 'keepers', not customers, found?
Why 'writs' and not business, appear to abound?
And the rich man, who toils not – the poor man, who digs,
Will answer 'The Curse – the Black Curse of the Whigs!'

Go forth to our quays – there is bustle indeed,
Thronging thousands your passage completely impede;
Childhood, youth, manhood, age, all the sinew and bone,
Of a nation from off her green bosom are thrown,
You ask why those thousands for ever have strayed,
From the knolls where their forefathers' ashes are laid;
And the rich man, who toils not – the poor man, who digs,
Will answer 'The Curse – the Black Curse of the Whigs!'

And go – oh pray go if your patience can brook,
The poor degradation to please a French cook,
To the scene of his triumph – their utter disgrace,
Their bitterest tears – his most smirking grimace,
See the animals up to their feeding troughs called,
And ask, why are hearts sorrow-laden thus galled?
And the rich man, who toils not – the poor man, who digs,
Will answer 'The Curse – the Black Curse of the Whigs!'

Oh! Like a black cloud, despair-laden, it looms,
And millions to death it has doomed, and still dooms;
And a plentiful crop to the graveyard it yields,
Although it denies any seed to the fields!
And a harvest it brings to the Bankruptcy Court,

Although it denies to the trader support,
Oh! o'er him, who toils not – and o'er him, who digs,
Is darkly impending – 'The Curse of the Whigs!'[18]

3

WORST FEARS REALISED

As August 1846 progressed it became apparent that the people's worst fears were being realised with news that the entire potato crop was failing. On mainland Europe widespread crop failures were forcing up the price of other food harvests. Trevelyan had called for the public work schemes to be shut down in July, and there was very little protest from the Irish members of parliament. Trevelyan had a number of reasons for this proposal, the main one being that he did not want the Irish famine affecting costs in England as the country was experiencing an industrial depression. The government was reluctant to invest too much financial support for Ireland, and Trevelyan agreed with this decision. He felt that it was unfair for English or Scottish labourers to pay higher food prices, which might be expected if any financial support was given to Ireland.[1] Reports on the new crops were not very favourable, and Trevelyan knew that if government relief was still available when news spread that the potato harvest was failing, then people would 'expect to be fed' by the government.[2]

By November 1846, with food prices on the increase, a labourer would have to earn 21 shillings per week to sustain an average family of six or eight. However, the wages were only 6 or 8 shillings per week – even if one could find work on a relief scheme. This meant that families would continually grow more and more malnourished, resulting in a slow process of starvation and death. Initially, the men were paid by the day, but some employers, particularly large farmers, complained that this might cause workers to slow down to make the job last longer. Some schemes also found it difficult to pay workers on time, and some men had to wait to be paid until finance became available. In the meantime, they would have to purchase food on credit from dealers who took full advantage of the situation by charging exorbitant prices, knowing that it was eat or die for the workers and their families. Sadly, this happened with increasing regularity throughout the famine period. These dealers became known as 'Gombeen Men', a term which, over time, evolved into a different meaning in the west of Ireland, where it described someone a bit foolish.

Because of the risk of death to thousands of peasants, the relief works were allowed to continue at an average wage of 1 shilling per day. Cattle and sheep farmers had to guard their herds from people desperate for food. As the famine progressed, pigs and chickens disappeared – all were eaten. Other animals, such as donkeys, horses and even dogs were also eaten, as were all species of wild bird. Extracting blood from cattle, being careful not to endanger the life of the animal, also provided sustenance. The blood was then mixed with vegetables and baked on an open fire. It was a very welcome meal for the hungry, and some say it resulted in the old saying, 'Hunger is a good sauce.' In the fields and wooded areas, nettles, various roots, berries, nuts, mushrooms and even dandelions all became part of the daily diet for the starving.[3] Examples of this are recorded in the following chapters. Fishing was not an option for most people, and in fact many fishermen were as dependent on the potato as everyone else. The boats that were available were not capable of fishing far from shore, and it was also reported that for some reason fish shoals seem to have remained distant from shore during those years.[4] However, equipment was the major issue, and in many cases it was sold to provide food. Shellfish and edible seaweed supplies were exhausted quickly as people became increasingly desperate.[5] There was also the danger of eating the wrong type of shellfish or seaweed, as was the particular case of Pat and Bridget Duffy, a brother and sister who lived near Spiddal in County Galway. The only 'food' that they could find during the days prior to their deaths was 'sea-grass and sea-weed', and they were found dead shortly afterwards.[6] Before the famine, most people avoided eating shellfish and other seashore food and were ignorant of dangerous varieties or how it should be cooked. Because of this, many people all around the coast died because of either not cooking the food properly or eating the wrong seafood.[7] Freshwater fishing was also off limits to the peasants as the landlords owned most of the rivers and the poaching laws were always strictly enforced.[8]

Among those who witnessed the disaster unfolding and saw at first hand the desperation of the people was Fr Theobald Mathew, the famous temperance priest. In a letter to Trevelyan, in 1846, he warned that a blast had passed over the land and the food of a whole nation had perished. During a journey to Dublin he said that the crops he saw looked healthy. However, upon his return to Cork a few days later he witnessed many frightened and wretched people crying bitterly over their decaying gardens of 'putrefying vegetation' and the 'destruction that had left them foodless'.[9] This seems to have been the case in many places; initially the crops seemed good, giving hope to the people, but this optimism was short-lived as news of the second crop failure spread. It was greeted with anger and despair as people gathered in towns and villages throughout the country. Protest marches took place in many areas such as Skibbereen and Macroom, County Cork, and in Killarney, County Kerry. On 22 August 1846, hundreds of people had marched on the home of Lord Sligo in Westport, County Mayo, to protest and to emphasise the shocking situation now facing them. These protests were not aimed at upheaval but rather at highlighting the absolute despair and suffering of a hungry people. Of course there were those who broke the law, but they did so out of pure desperation, and mainly non-violent crimes occurred.[10] Many people simply broke the law to gain access to prison where they were sure of a meal.

There were some exceptions to the rule. In Connemara, County Galway, a boy was murdered on his way home with rations that he had collected from a relief store near Costello Lodge. A man viciously attacked him with a blunt object, beat him to death and robbed him of his meagre rations. A young girl died having been attacked in Renmore, Galway. It seems that either she or someone of her family was caught taking some crops from a neighbouring field.[11]

For many, the only hope of sustenance was entering the dreaded workhouse. The country had been divided into unions by the Poor Law Act of 1838; this resulted in a workhouse being erected in each union. The poor-law system at the time did not allow for public assistance in times of distress unless people became inmates of the workhouse.[12] Conditions in the workhouse were deliberately harsh; this was to deter any 'able-bodied' poor from relying on the system. Husbands were separated from their wives upon entering the workhouse, and parents were separated from their children. They also had to surrender their own clothing or rags and wear a distinctive workhouse uniform. The treatment in the workhouse was in many ways similar to that in prisons, leaving many inmates feeling that they were being punished for the 'crime of poverty'. The conditions suffered in some workhouses led to depression among adults and children alike. While there were many well-meaning measures such as education for children and the appointment of doctors and chaplains, most workhouses were run on a shoestring budget, causing these benevolent gestures to fall well short of their target, particularly during the famine.[13] The food in many workhouses was also dreadful, but it was the only means of nourishment for a desperate population. Much of the time it was prepared in a fever-ridden environment and was itself the cause of sickness.

As desperation set in, hundreds of children were left behind by families leaving the country. Many parents did not have enough money to pay for passage for all the family members. It was hoped in many cases that they would earn enough money abroad to be in a position to send for their child or children later. However, many of these children died before they could be reunited with their families.[14] Many children were found to be

The Skibbereen Road. (*The Illustrated London News*, 1847)

suffering from smallpox, whooping cough and measles. Starving children also suffered from ophthalmia, which caused blindness. Some diseases were airborne, but some were also associated with lice and, given that people were living in such terrible conditions and in close proximity to each other, this caused serious problems.[15] Other parents simply abandoned their children in the workhouse as they felt that it was the only hope of survival for them. Workhouses throughout Ireland were soon overwhelmed by the scale of the disaster, with people arriving daily begging to be admitted.

There were some benevolent organisations such as the Society of Friends, or the Quakers as they are more commonly known, who came to the aid of the people. These were kind and compassionate people, and they did all they could to alleviate the suffering of the peasants. They also helped local communities by supplying equipment to support those in need. They set up soup kitchens in many areas.

The food distributed at soup kitchens was intended strictly for the infirm and the destitute unemployed. However, there were abuses of the system, with some areas claiming more assistance than was required for their community. The soup, known as 'stirabout', was made from a mixture of Indian corn and rice boiled together. Some recipes contained meat, which was a real bonus for those lucky enough to secure a bowl of this nourishment. However, in some areas the soup was ill-prepared and caused sicknesses such as diarrhoea. Other food issued consisted of flour, bread and biscuits and was rationed according to age, with adults obviously receiving larger portions than children. While the system worked reasonably well, some people were reluctant to face the humiliation of standing in a line to receive food. In contrast, others fought and roared at each other to get to the front of the queue.

The Quaker soup kitchens were the best run outlets as they were not interested in the politics or religious beliefs of the people in need; for them, helping the starving masses was the priority. However, others took advantage of the situation for religious purposes. It was reported that Catholics living in Connemara were being offered soup if they would agree to change their religion and become Protestant, but these offers were made at privately run soup kitchens.[16] This has cast a shadow over the relief work carried out by these particular clergymen and the women who helped them, and has caused a degree of humiliation in Irish folk memory.[17] It is believed that most of the peasant Catholics who availed themselves of this offer simply assumed the new religion temporarily to survive and to secure food and shelter for their children.[18]

The soup kitchens were feeding some 3 million people a day, and the cost proved too great for them to continue. The finance was supposed to be provided by local landlords and ratepayers, which proved impossible to collect as the famine progressed. The poor-law unions were in serious financial difficulties because of the huge debts that were mounting against them. This led to the closure of the soup-kitchen scheme in September 1847; bleak was the year and worse was to come.[19] The following poem appeared in *The Galway Vindicator* in October 1847:

The Poor Man's Harvest: A Dirge

The earth with abundance is teeming,
The fruitage is thick on the tree,
And hope in the distance is beaming,
But Paddy, alas! not for thee,
In vain the great Lord of the harvest,
Among us his blessings has sent,
For still my poor fellow thou cravest,
The poor wretched rations of Lent.

There's mirth on the hill and the heather,
There's joy through the wood and the world,
The wild birds are happy together,
The lambkins rejoice in the fold,
The farmer smiles over his harvest,
The Landlord gloats over his rent,

Poor Paddy, poor fellow, thou cravest,
The still wretched rations of Lent.

There's grain for the ox and the garran,
There's food for the dog and the swine,
There's bread for the bishop and baron,
The Peer has his turtle and wine,
But he who has gathered the harvest,
The man, neath the toll has bent,
Poor Paddy, God help thee, thou starvest,
Still on the poor rations of Lent.

But autumn is fast fading from us,
The winter is dark at the door,
It comes without hope, without promise,
And bleak blows the blast on the moor,
But my poor Pat where is thy harvest?
And where the fat pig for thy rent?
All gone, while the tyrant thou servest,
But leaves thee the rations of Lent.

In hunger thy children are pining,
Rude, ragged and rueful they roam,
For them there's no supping – no dining,
No hearth, nor the comforts of home,
For them, wirra struagh! There's no harvest,
Their slavery is never unbent,
While crushed and heart-broken, thou starvest,
Upon the poor rations of Lent.

Great patience to thee hath been given,
Thy breast with forbearance is strong,
Or thou would'st uprise before Heaven,
And wreak the oppressors their wrong,
But he who makes fruitful the harvest,
May yet cause thy foes to repent,
Tho' now neath their bondage thou starvest,
In all the privations of Lent.[20]

4

FAMINE STRIKES GALWAY

Outbreaks of famine were not uncommon in Ireland during the eighteenth and nineteenth centuries. The severe winter of 1739 was followed by almost two years of famine and disease in which many of the poor perished. Consignments of ship biscuits were attacked and seized as they were being loaded onto ships at the Galway quay. Horrific scenes were reported from around the country, where it was said that the dead were eaten in the fields by dogs for want of people to bury them. The west of Ireland always suffered during times of want and trouble. During these times its capital, Galway, was besieged with refugees fleeing famine. The fact that it was a port town also attracted people as it was a means of escape for those who could afford passage to another country. Between 1740 and 1741, the town itself became one 'large lazaretto with thousands of people dying in the streets from fever and bloody flux'.[1]

The problems did not end there; food shortages were again reported in 1816 and 1817. In 1822, the town was suffering severely from the effects of high unemployment and poverty, and the failure of the potato crop that year caused a minor famine. Hordes of people flocked into the town in search of food, but the authorities already had problems feeding their own population. There were so many people suffering from the severe effects of hunger during that summer that fever became widespread. Because of this, grants were made available to combat the epidemic, and by November the scourge seemed to have passed. Other food shortages occurred in 1831 and 1842; the latter year saw food riots in Galway city where potato stores were attacked. However, the catastrophe that swept across Ireland in 1845 could not be compared to anything the country had ever witnessed before.[2]

Initially, it was business as usual; after all, as mentioned already, the town was no stranger to food shortages, and at first the situation did not seem to be any worse than usual. In October 1845, the Royal Agricultural Improvement Society held a banquet in Ballinasloe. Among the speakers was the Earl of Devon, who announced to the gathering of landlords and landowners that the 'condition' of the Irish people was improving. In order to denounce newspaper reports about the state of the country, he also stated that the Irish press 'should endeavour to advocate the interest of the empire rather than the interests of Ireland, that ... Ireland should imitate England, the proudest nation on the face of the earth.'[3] This was met with great approval from all those present, who were indulging themselves in the 'choicest viands and rarest delicacies of the sea', washed down with wine, champagne and claret of the richest vintage. With such open indifference, it is little wonder that landlords' agents, bailiffs and a whole 'host of understrappers' were to be found prowling among the 'wretched tenements' seeking rents from the poverty-stricken people in that same town.

However, people began to worry upon seeing food stocks leaving the port of Galway. A mass meeting was held in Loughrea to try to discourage farmers and merchants from allowing their wheat and other provisions to leave the area. The police inspector in Loughrea warned the authorities that looting would result unless relief was forthcoming for the people who were now on the brink of starvation. His warnings were ignored; this was only the beginning, and nothing was going to stop the export of food.[4] The police barracks in Abbeygate Street, Galway, was also put on alert. Both the chief inspector, Isidore Blake, and the sub-inspector, John Lynch, were from Prospect Hill, and, being local men, they were very concerned as they were familiar with the people of the town.[5] Their warnings were also ignored, including the following notice which was posted on the walls of Galway Gashouse in January 1846. This site was chosen because it was the main venue for the town commissioners' meetings. This was a serious warning, one could say close on anarchic, regarding the export of corn out of the town:

> Notice; Is hereby given that we want the Town Commissioners to put a stop to corn and keep in this Town unless you do we give fair warning in spite of priests and Bishops that we will break and smash all the Stores and Cellars in Town and rob and steal both day and night Hour and minute that we can the parcell of robbers and Watchmen that ye have robbin the rich and poor all hours of the night may venture to enroll our names that knows the B from a bulls foot and then we will get a loaf of bread this 19th day of January 1846.[6]

As the months progressed, it became evident that the situation was going to be much worse than people had previously thought. While Galway was not the worst-hit area during the famine, it did suffer greatly with its share of disease, starvation and death.

Many deaths occurred in the workhouse on Newcastle Road. The Galway workhouse had opened on 3 March 1842, the same year as the food riots in the town, and the first person to be admitted was an old and infirm man who died shortly afterwards.[7] Most of the inmates were destitute, people who could not find employment or who were unable to work because of illness. The vast majority of people tried to avoid such places but extreme circumstances forced many of them to seek shelter in the workhouse.[8] Most workhouses had a distinctive uniform; the Galway workhouse issued women with canvas dresses, and while this was a very coarse material it was far better than the rags that barely covered their emaciated bodies upon admittance. It seems that suppliers were invited to submit tenders at the beginning of each year, but even such cost awareness made little or no difference to the situation, as resources were drained because of the numbers requiring support.[9] The average cost of housing an inmate was 8½ pence per week.[10] The workhouse staff at the time included Mr Coghlan, supervisor; Dr Browne, medical examiner; John Corcoran in administration; and Fr Peter Daly to attend to the spiritual needs of the inmates. There were many others employed, and staff members continually changed during the famine years.[11]

Fr Daly became one of the most controversial priests of the nineteenth century and was involved in all aspects of life in

Galway. While he had many critics, he seems to have been a very benevolent priest during the famine period. He warned the relief committee in 1846 that he had hundreds of parishioners in grave danger of starvation and that some of them had not eaten in days. He stated that he would give them the 'coat off his back' if it would help but that there were just too many people in need. Some 45,000 people, a quarter of the population in his parish area, were already dependent on public charity.[12] The population had greatly increased with the influx of starving people.

Another building used to house the poor during this time was the fever hospital on Earl's Island, located just opposite the New Cathedral, close to Beggar's Bridge. This hospital had opened during the 1820s; it was small and similar to the workhouse, and it proved very inadequate as the extent of the disaster unfolded. According to some sources, inmates from the fever hospital and the workhouse would beg for food or assistance on the bridge close by, hence the name 'Beggar's Bridge'.[13]

A local relief committee had been set up in Galway during March 1846. It comprised members of the clergy and prominent citizens of the town, and they would supervise work schemes and organise the distribution of food. A ship loaded with maize and corn arrived into Galway dock in June 1846. It was immediately secured in government stores located close to the quay until it could be distributed in an orderly manner to the people of the town and outlying districts.[14] Funds required for the planned work schemes were also held in secure locations, the main one being the Bank of Ireland on Eyre Square in Galway. During the famine this bank played the most important role in its history, acting as the main distribution centre for famine relief funds in Connacht.[15] In August 1846, the first of the relief funds arrived in Galway docks on board *HMS Commet*. The sum amounted to £80,000 and was welcomed by the local authorities.[16]

In order for a man to be employed on the relief schemes, he had to have a 'work ticket', and some 8,400 men in the city were ticket holders. The public relief works in Galway included the construction of Threadneedle Road (then called Bóthar na Mine) and the Dyke Road. Unlike some public works in other parts of the country, the schemes in Galway city were constructive in the sense that the work was beneficial to the town. The Dyke Road initiative, for example, banked off the River Corrib which up until that period was constantly overflowing its banks and flooding the surrounding area. Work was also carried out on roads in Rahoon, Salthill, Shantalla, Ballybrit and the Headford Road area. There were seven deaths from hunger recorded among the workers; one of them was Patrick Lardner who died because a pay clerk on the works scheme had not paid him for fifteen days and he had no money to purchase food.[17]

Manpower was also required to work on the new railway line being planned for the Galway-to-Dublin route. The work went ahead, providing a few years' employment, until finally, on 26 July 1851 the Midland Great Western Railway officially opened without ceremony, as the directors felt even at that time that any such festivities would be a useless outlay of money. Once the work had begun, the authorities in Galway suggested that men from the town and county should be employed working on the railway west of the Shannon rather than men from other parts of the country.[18] Its construction gave much-needed employment, as did the building of Galway Railway Station and the huge bridge over Lough Atalia, the sea inlet and road.[19]

The building of Queen's College Galway (now the National University of Ireland, Galway) provided further employment during the famine years. Two other colleges were also being built, one in Cork and the other in Belfast. However, Archbishop MacHale of Tuam directed his anger against the building of these 'infidel' and 'Godless colleges' because they were non-religious. They were the main target of criticism in his Lenten pastoral letter in March 1846. In the letter he instructed the faithful to 'fast' and not to accept employment on these buildings. One wonders about such comments given that the peasantry was already suffering from the effects of an unwanted 'fast'.[20] Nevertheless, a year later his attitude had changed, and he strongly condemned the authorities for their lack of support with regard to public works and the payment schemes, stating, 'I have found the people, owing to the ignorance, or carelessness, or inhumanity of officials, exposed to starvation.'[21]

The worsening conditions also led to an enormous increase in prisoners in Galway jail as many destitute people sought refuge there by committing petty crime. One case in particular was of a woman and child who entered lands at Frenchfort, near Oranmore, and killed a sheep belonging to John Ryan Esq. When apprehended, the unfortunate woman said that she had committed the crime to gain access to Galway jail where she and her child would be fed.[22]

In the midst of all this hardship, evictions began to increase, adding to an already difficult situation. In March 1846, at Ballinglass, County Galway, seventy-six families, comprising

The village of Tullig, County Clare. (*The Illustrated London News*, 1849)

some 300 tenants, were evicted from the Gerrard Estate. This exercise was carried out with the assistance of police and troops. These people were willing to pay the rent as they had the money, but this did not save them; the landlord simply wished to turn their holdings into grazing land. The families found some shelter in ditches along the roadside and erected temporary coverings to protect themselves from the elements, but they were also driven 'mercilessly' from these places of refuge. In June, the relief committee at Clonrush obtained £65 from the Lord Lieutenant to try to help a 'myriad of squatters' who had also been evicted. He was informed that there were 236 families consisting of 1,307 individuals, all of whom were unemployed and without provisions, and that many of them would soon become victims of the famine. It was happening all around the county; in Clifden help was sought for 4,000 destitute families who had been turned out of their homes, many of whom were now ill having consumed contaminated meal.[23]

As 1846 drew to a close, it was evident that thousands would not survive the winter unless there was a concerted effort by all concerned to help feed the poor. In Galway, as in many other areas, responsibility mainly fell upon local organisations to try to combat the disaster. In December 1846, a Protestant clergyman, Revd John D'Arcy, had the first soup kitchen set up in Back Street. The Dominican Fathers set up another soup kitchen in the Claddagh. All the religious orders united in a bid to alleviate the scourge of hunger, and by May 1847 some sixteen soup kitchens were in operation around the town.[24] A soup kitchen was also set up at Barna, a village some five miles west of the city on the coast road. It was mainly supported by the Sisters of Mercy. The sisters also helped dispense soup amongst the poor of the area who were unable to come to the depot. Fr Peter Daly was involved in this establishment and secured financial support from wealthy landowners, Nicholas Lynch of Barna and Marcus Lynch of Paris. Incidentally, the cook was French and by all accounts the food and soup were of a high standard.[25] This soup kitchen kept hundreds alive; each meal consisted of a large bowl of meat soup and 12 ounces of bread. The soup contained vegetables, rice, oatmeal and meat.

The soup kitchens combined were feeding some 7,500 people every day in the town. Local businesses and individuals donated most of the food provided. The kitchens were located at the Presentation Convent, the Convent of Mercy, St Vincent's Convent, Taylor's Hill, Merchant's Road and Lombard Street. The price of the meal in the soup kitchens was 1½ pence, but those who could not afford the meal did not go away hungry. A food depot was also set up by the Quakers in Merchants Road, and they distributed provisions and clothing to the needy and to the Orphans' Breakfast Institute, which was set up by Brother Paul O'Connor of the Old Monastery School in Lombard Street. The situation deteriorated even more when Connemara children, driven by hunger, made their way to this school. A consignment of maize arrived in Galway in November 1846, and, while this was a welcome contribution, it would only keep hunger at bay for a short time.[26]

To help support women and children, the Widows' and Orphans' Asylum was set up on College Road. It had a number of subscribers, one of whom was Charles Bianconi, of Bianconi transport.[27] During Christmas 1846, Fr Peter Daly personally purchased enough food to feed 100 families in the Barna area. Oscar Henry Oustaing wrote the following famine poem in December 1846 in Galway:

THE POOR MAN'S CHRISTMAS:
A CAROL FOR THE YEAR OF FAMINE

Sad is the Christmas of the Poor Man, and lonely,
Not one single comfort his misery to soften,
He no longer can dig that food which, ah, only,
Has saved him from starving, so long and so often!

Oh! cheerless and cold is the poor Peasant's dwelling,
Black and lonely it stands on the black mountain's side,
The heart of its owner with anguish is swelling,
For the food – for the fire – that he cannot provide!

Christmas for the wealthy, 1848. (*The Illustrated London News*, 1848)

No smoke from the roof of his cabin of sorrow,
In blue wreaths is mirror'd by the clear sparkling rills,
No fire can be got till the market tomorrow,
For the load is bright heath he must bring from the hills.

Wild, wistful he looks on the cold hearth before him,
And turns to his children – half famish'd and crying –
As he kneels to the Lord, to faintly implore Him,
To save his dear babes and their mother from dying!

Och, och, children machree! he convulsively cries,
Try to sleep, darlin's, do! and be sobbin' no more,
Och, there, Maureen, mavourneen! there dry now your eyes,
Or my heart will be breaking ma colleen astore!

Oh, the glance it was ghastly their sunk eyes express'd,
As they clung round his knees, his kind comforts to seek,
While his Maureen, so loved – on his breast,
Try'd to smile, as she kiss'd the soft tear from his cheek!

Yes, she smil'd, but the smile was the offspring of sadness,
Oh, unlike the heart's rays when our day-dreams are fair,
Like the maniac's laugh, the laugh still of madness,
So she smil'd, but her smile was the smile of Despair!

Thus the beautiful bird, which tho dying will sing,
Tho' expiring, it breathes its own funeral strains!
As the sweet scented flower, which blooms in the spring,
Tho' tis broken and trampled, its fragrance remains!

Oh, my God! that the hour of redemption – relief –
As that glad festive hour which we hail with delight,
Should find the poor peasant in the darkness of grief,
And his heart wrapt in want and affliction's long night!

So, tis, and gaunt Famine the poor man's reviling,
His children are starving, his own heart is breaking,
While all things around him rejoice and are smiling,
He sleeps on in mis'ry that knows no waking![28]

5

A BRUTAL WINTER

The day-to-day administration of Galway city was the respon-sibility of the town commissioners. They included James Davis (Chairman), D. Darcy (Secretary), Pat Cummins, Constantine Sloper, Michael McNamara, John Holland, L. S. Mangan, L. Geoghegan, T. Murray, A. R. Mullins, James Stephens, Arthur Ireland, John Hart and Joseph Grealy.[1] Nineteenth-century employment in the town was more or less centred on the various mills and businesses located along the banks of the River Corrib. There was always a strong tradition of milling in Galway, dating from the foundation of the city. The river was the main contributing factor for such trade, so it was not unusual to find seven 'industrial estates' with various types of mills working away throughout the nineteenth century. The name of Mill Street, located close to the waterways, is a testament to this industry. The river supported three flour mills on Presentation Road while at Newtownsmith there were three more flour mills, an oat and bark mill and a distillery.[2]

It is interesting to note that there were at least three whiskey distilleries in Galway during the famine. Obviously business interests continued as best they could in the town. One of them,

Burke's Distillery, seems to have opened about the time of the famine. It was located on the site of the present-day Jury's Hotel and was more commonly known at the time as the 'Quarter Barrel Distillery'. Burton Persse of Newcastle House owned two distilleries, one in Newcastle and another in Newtownsmith. He purchased another one, Joyce's Distillery on Nun's Island, in 1840. However, a short time later he closed the Newtownsmith business and concentrated all of his efforts on the Nun's Island Distillery. Persse was a member of an ascendancy family who had properties throughout County Galway. His houses included Roxborough House, most famous as the birthplace of Isabella Augusta Persse, who later became Lady Gregory of Coole. Persse's Nun's Island business provided good employment, with at least 100 people working there during the famine, giving them some degree of security.

A number of smaller businesses also benefited from the mills and distilleries. While all of these industries provided what would have been considered a large workforce during normal times, this proved totally inadequate during the famine because of the numbers arriving in Galway almost daily seeking work. Something more would have to be done to create employment.[3]

On 1 December 1846, the Galway Industrial Society was founded. The purpose of the society was to provide employment for women in the town and the surrounding districts. The authorities had complained that there were hundreds of women spending their days in 'utter idleness' simply because there was no work provided for them, nor were they being encouraged to find employment. The work of the society involved the spinning and knitting of garments such as stockings, shirts, blankets and

Scalpeen (refuge) near Kilrush, County Clare.
(*The Illustrated London News*, 1849)

nightcaps. The manager of the National Bank, Mr Hyde, and a wealthy Galway lady, Mrs Gray, extended finance towards the venture, which saw an immediate success. Many of the goods were exported to the USA, where several markets had agreed to take the commodities. The society also promoted the idea of people purchasing locally manufactured goods rather than imported merchandise. While the society experienced initial success, it required substantial funds to expand and survive in the American market. Unfortunately, the support required was not forthcoming, and only limited employment could be given – and this could not be guaranteed indefinitely.[4]

Another problem for the town was that between June 1845 and June 1846 the cost of cereals and animal products trebled on the Galway market, making it difficult even for those working on relief schemes to purchase foodstuffs.[5] The work on these schemes was hard and the hours were long; much of it involved breaking stone with the aid of a small hammer. A healthy man could earn a shilling a day, but most were weak and were only earning 8 pence.[6] The work was particularly tough in areas outside the town where men and boys had to walk many miles each day on empty stomachs to support their families. Many died working on these schemes.

One man who fell victim to this relief work was Thomas Mollone. In November 1846 he was working on the Costello Bay to Oughterard road for some four weeks. He had to walk six miles each morning over a wet, pathless mountainside and faced the same journey home each evening. The job involved carrying heavy wet sand packs on his back all day with little in his stomach, which proved a brutal task. He had no choice but to struggle on, as he had to earn money to keep his wife and six children alive. One evening, he was so weakened by hunger and fatigue that he lay down to rest close to his home and died. He was just one of many who did not survive.[7]

Adding to the misery facing the people, the brutal winter of 1846–7 was the worst in living memory. There was continuous snow and blizzards, which lasted until April 1847. The fierce weather conditions, along with inadequate clothing, proved fatal for many destitute people who could not gain access to the workhouse. By January 1847, the workhouse in Galway, which had been designed to cater for 800 inmates, was now struggling to house 1,300 people. The number of deaths averaged between twenty-five and thirty people per week.[8] Later in the year, auxiliary workhouses were opened in Newtownsmith, Merchants Road, Barna and Dangan. The one at Dangan was on a one-acre site, and the authorities secured it for three years at £145 per year; the complex could accommodate 600 'paupers'.[9] In addition to this, accommodation for orphaned children was provided at Parkavera, Dangan and Moycullen. Around the county, other buildings were being converted into accommodation for the poor, such as in Loughrea, where a local brewery was requisitioned for this purpose.[10]

However, these places of refuge were not opened in time for the thousands suffering in January 1847, and, even if they had been available, they would not have been sufficient such was the scale of the disaster now unfolding. It was common to find bodies lying in ditches along the side of the road, some with grass-stained mouths bearing testament to their desperation. It was once said of the district of Rahoon that no language could express the ghastly suffering of the poor and destitute during the famine. It was reported that 'on every side nothing but cries of death and starvation are heard. The poor are literally dropping on the public highways from hunger.'[11] Other frightening reports of the 'awful ravages of famine' were spreading around the town and the county. *The Galway Mercury* stated:

Again, and again, the painful duty devolves upon us to record the awful ravages of Famine. Turn we to the North or to the South,

69

to the East or to the West, the mournful cry of desolation comes upon our ears, proclaiming the melancholy state of destitution to which thousands of our countrymen are now unhappily reduced. Where then shall we begin our fearful tale of misery and woe? Every locality of this district abounds in cases too horrible for the human heart to dwell upon without emotion, and but too sadly indicating the awful and widespread ruin that has come upon the land.[12]

Cattle and sheep driven between Oughterard and Galway.
(*The Illustrated London News*, 1849)

Unforgettable scenes of human misery were witnessed in the surrounding areas. There were reports of the bodies of women and children lying in ditches along the Dangan and Barna roads. One of the women found on the Dangan road was Mary Commons, who died while making her way to the workhouse.

Her case is interesting as some jurors attending her inquest held the government directly responsible and wanted them charged and brought to justice. The day before she died she had called to the home of Mark and Mary Carr in the village of Ballagh, about two miles from Galway city. She was a frequent visitor to the house, and on this occasion she asked for a drink of water. The Carr family was not in a position to give Mary any food, as they were almost as poor as she was herself. However, the head of the household, Mark Carr, did the best he could for Mary and added milk to a cup of water to try and give her some nourishment. She did not stay with them very long as she was anxious to get to the workhouse as early as possible to try and gain admission. The following day, 13 January 1847, John Corcoran from the workhouse was making his way to Dangan when he came across the body of Mary Commons lying on the side of the road. There were several women standing around her, saddened by the sight before them. Upon investigation he discovered in her pocket 3 pence, rosary beads, a pipe and tobacco; these few items represented all her worldly possessions. He had the body taken to the workhouse where the Medical Examiner, Dr Browne, carried out a post-mortem. During the inquest, Dr Browne stated that the deceased woman's stomach and intestines were 'perfectly empty'. While the coroner was recording his verdict, several jurors interrupted him and gave their own verdict:

We find, that the deceased, Mary Commons, died from the effects of starvation and destitution, caused by a want of the common necessities of life; and as Lord John Russell, the head of her Majesty's

71

Government, has combined with Sir Randolph Routh, to starve the Irish people, by not as was their duty, taking measures to prevent the present truly awful condition of the country WE FIND THAT THE SAID LORD JOHN RUSSELL AND THE SAID SIR RANDOLPH ROUTH, ARE GUILTY OF THE WILFUL MURDER OF THE SAID MARY COMMONS.[13]

These two men were publicly named many times as being responsible for the deaths of people during the famine. Another case involved a lady named Lawless from Rahoon who collapsed from starvation at Taylor's Hill and, despite the best efforts of the Dominican nuns in the convent close by, died. *The Galway Mercury* declared that she was added to 'the list of victims sacrificed to the insane starvation policy of Lord John Russell and Sir Randolph Routh. Another human being has been thus sent to great account by these heartless statesmen.'[14]

Reports such as these can be found throughout the country, and one can easily see why these men were being blamed for the suffering; after all, little was done to stop foodstuffs being exported out of a country where hundreds of people were now starving to death daily. They were in a position of power and responsibility, and, as far as the Irish people were concerned, they were simply not doing enough to alleviate the terrible conditions that had developed in Ireland.[15] The following letter was written as a criticism of Lord John Russell in October 1846. It also highlights the rising price of the potato and the broken promises made by the government:

Heretofore we have been anticipating the approach of famine. We have now, alas, to announce its actual existence in this town. We had hoped that the unremitting exertions of the inhabitants would have prevented, or mitigated, the awful effects of the calamity which has befallen our people, and that an administration, which boasted of its anxiety to save the starving millions of Ireland, would have taken bold and decided steps for that purpose. We find ourselves mistaken; and famine, absolute famine, with its gaunt and dreary attendants, sickness and death, has truly and really come among us … What, then, is to become of our people? Prices are every day rising; within the last few days they have reached a famine figure, fully twenty per cent above those of last week, and yet we will be told to be patient, to be quiet, to be submissive and docile; not to raise a cry of complaint.[16]

Lord John Russell had become the Prime Minister of Great Britain in June 1846 when he replaced Robert Peel. Russell's Whig administration believed that Irish wealth should alleviate Irish poverty. It rejected the policy of direct state intervention or aid for Ireland and wanted the landlords to shoulder the responsibility. This policy proved fatal for thousands of peasants. The poor-law unions that had been set up to combat the problems were unable to cope with the burden of a growing starving population.

In January 1847 Russell's administration was forced to modify its non-interventionist policy and it made some finance available for relief, but this was only on loan and was not sufficient to cope with the disaster at hand. While the potato crop did not fail in 1847, the yield was extremely low. This resulted in hundreds of thousands of starving people pouring into towns and cities across the country seeking relief. Epidemics of typhoid fever, cholera and dysentery broke out and claimed more lives than starvation itself. In September 1847 Russell's government ended what little relief it had made available; it demanded that the poor-law rates be collected before any further financial support would be made available. The collection of these rates in a period of extreme hardship caused widespread unrest and violence. Some 16,000 extra British troops were sent to Ireland, and troubled parts of the country were placed under martial law.[17]

The other man named by the jurors as being responsible was

Judy O'Donnell and her family shelter under a bridge at Doonbeg. (*The Illustrated London News*, 1849)

Sir Randolph Routh; he was the Commissary-General for Relief in Ireland and took the government stance on relief. This is obvious from a meeting he had with a delegation from Achill, County Mayo, in the autumn of 1846. The delegation explained that because of the high prices merchants were being charged, the people were simply not in a position to purchase corn. When they asked him to have the price of the corn reduced, he replied that it was essential to the success of commerce that the mercantile interest should not be interfered with. The leader of the delegation, Fr Monahan, reminded him that during the previous year the government had sold it at a cheaper rate to keep the price lower. Routh responded saying that this had been a mistake as it had given people 'bad habits', and he also said that the government was now determined not to interfere with the merchants but to act in accordance with the 'enlightened principles of political economy'. The result of the government's persistence with regard to its policy was to prove catastrophic for the Irish people.[18]

Another man whose name became renowned in connection with the suffering of the people was Sir William Gregory of Coole Park near Gort in County Galway. His name is still remembered for the infamous 'Gregory Clause'. He proposed this clause when he was Member of Parliament for Dublin. Gregory was trying to ensure that undeserving persons should not get relief. He proposed an amendment to the Poor Law Act of 1847 which stated that anyone possessing more than a quarter of an acre of land should not be entitled to assistance.[19] The proposal became law and was known as the 'Gregory Clause'. This resulted in small tenant farmers and their families being forced off the land as they could not get assistance while they were living on their holdings. They only way they could qualify for support was if they had no other means of support. The only option for many of them was the poorhouse or the coffin ship. Over the following months, vast numbers of smallholders surrendered their land to qualify for assistance. Once the family left their cabin, it was generally pulled down by the landlord's agent and his men, thus making them permanent paupers.[20]

By 1848, this law had taken a brutal toll around the country-side. A gentleman travelling through a 'scene of extermination' near Kinvara at that time reported that on both sides of the road he had witnessed many houses in ruins, from which the occupants had been expelled. These homes were on the property of William Gregory. Shortly afterwards *The Galway Vindicator* published what was seen as a favourable article regarding Gregory, who was planning for an election campaign in Galway. There was much unrest over this, and the *Limerick Chronicle* came out strongly against it, given that similar 'exterminations' were also continuous in the south of Ireland. The Galway news-paper then had to retract its earlier support, and, to redeem its credibility, it published the following:

> On no occasion would we be understood as aiding this gentleman's pretensions as a candidate so long as he maintains his well known bigoted and conservative principles. He is, besides, the author of the Quarter-Acre Gregory clause, and if our intelligence be correct, is now actively executing its intentions.[21]

While this report casts a rather dreadful light on Gregory's intentions, others seem to think that his objective was genuine. Regardless of his intentions, it proved disastrous for the tenants as it enabled unscrupulous landlords who wished to take advantage of the Act to clear their estates of surplus and unwanted tenants. The following poem was composed about the 'Gregory Clause' and appeared in *The Galway Mercury* in 1849:

GREGORY'S QUARTER ACRE

When ruthless tyrants work so sure,
To swamp with famine breaker,
The death surge tumbles o'er the poor.
In Gregory's Quarter Acre.

Bees are done up with smoke and fire,
The lot of famine's bleaker,
For famine feeds the funeral pyre,
In Gregory's Quarter Acre.

And comes, time when Death shall be,
The test of woe, to wake her,
And hell shall laugh a devilish glee,
At Gregory's Quarter Acre.

The widow weeps in vain to see,
The coffin's undertaker,
Whilst as he digs 'bad luck' says he,
To Gregory's Quarter Acre.

Courage, ye virtuous poor who live,
Unknown to peace or baker,
An hour shall come when hope shall give,
A fig for Gregory's Quarter Acre.

Then bear in mind, though dim today,
Your lot, your friends, your Maker,

Your crown is great, when passed away,
Old Gregory's Quarter Acre.

The tyrant man who made that law,
A land like ours to break her,
Say is vengeance made of straw,
When named the Quarter Acre.

Mercy will point to regions hot,
For those who forsake her,
Ye Gods! To Gregory grant this spot,
As his own Quarter Acre.[22]

6

STARVATION WITNESSED

William Forster and his son, also named William, both of whom were Quakers, began a tour of Connacht in January 1847. They were from Leeds in England, and their visit was on behalf of their own community to view 'first-hand' the desolation caused by the famine and to see if the dreadful reports coming from the west of Ireland were true. For William Forster Senior it was his second visit to Connacht; he had been there some years earlier and was shocked into disbelief at the extreme changes that had occurred between his visits. He had made many acquaintances among the Irish people, particularly in Connemara during his first visit, and so he was very aware of the plight of the people. Things were now terribly different from what he remembered of the 'wild Irish fun' he had experienced during his previous trip to the west. There had been a welcome in every house, and what little they had they had shared. But now there was nothing to share, the humour was replaced by a complete 'silliness' among the poverty-stricken poor. Both men were shocked into silence by the situation that now confronted them. The following extract is taken from the reports compiled by the Forsters. One of the first places they visited in County Galway was the village of Bunderagh in Connemara:

> One poor woman, whose cabin I had visited, said, 'there will be nothing for us but to lie down and die.' I tried to give her hope of English aid, but alas, her prophecy has been too true. Out of a population of 240, I found thirteen already dead from want. The survivors were like walking skeletons – the men gaunt and haggard, stamped with the livid mark of hunger – the children crying with pain – the women in some of the cabins too weak to stand.

On the way to Clifden, they came across 100 men engaged in famine-relief roadworks near Kylemore. Many of these men had to walk between five and seven miles every day to earn 4 shillings and 6 pence per week. They were employed in this 'back-breaking' stonework with only one meagre meal a day to sustain them. A policeman who was standing close by told the visitors that some of the men 'work till they fall over their tools' such was their weakened state.[1] They were told that some of the men had not tasted food for up to eighteen hours. They were amazed at the patience of these workers, some of whom had not been paid for five weeks owing to negligent mistakes on the part of relief officers. They were touched by the manner in which the workers received news that there was no money available to pay them at present; there was 'a patient, quiet look of despair' about them as they returned to their work. They had to keep working as there was nothing else for them to do except to hold on to their employment in the hope of payment soon.[2] Upon arriving in Clifden, the Forsters were immediately

The workhouse at Clifden, County Galway.
(*The Illustrated London News*, 1849)

confronted with news of a woman who had crawled into an outhouse close to where they were staying on the previous night and had died there alone. By the time she was discovered starving dogs had devoured part of her remains. That same evening they observed another corpse being conveyed through the streets in a wheelbarrow, pushed by a man crying out for support to bury the body.[3]

Local priest Eugene Coyne recorded in a letter that scarcely a day passed without two or three people being found dead. There were often between eight and ten corpses in the churchyard at one time for burial. They were carried there by people who themselves had all the appearances of 'skeletons rather than human beings'.[4] It was also reported that the population around Clifden was fast dying away for 'want of food' and that many people were being 'hurried' to their graves through utter destitution without so much as a funeral ceremony or a coffin. There were many cases of burials that took place without coffins. The desperation drove people to the extreme; one man struggled into the town and sold his shoes for the price of a meal. The weather conditions were terrible – it was freezing cold, with constant rain and sleet – so it is little wonder that the following morning his lifeless body was found in the streets. He was yet another example from hundreds of cases in the same locality.[5]

The following morning, the Forsters boarded their carriage and left for Galway. They witnessed more horrific sights of human misery along the route. As they journeyed through Connemara, the question on their minds was not how the people had died but rather how they had managed to live. They had expected a serious situation in Connacht, but nothing could have prepared them for the desolation that greeted them, 'for it defied all exaggeration'.[6]

In other reports from Connemara during the same period, details of almost unparalleled suffering emerge. A pitiful hovel in the village of Glann, just west of Oughterard, revealed an entire family of ten people dead, all lying in a heap of 'rottenness and putrefaction'. In another nearby hovel seven more people were found in the same state while four others were struggling in the last throes of agony. What had 'once been a human being was found crawling on the ground' of a third hut, trying to stay alive on a few turnip peels that were not fit for the 'beasts of the field'.[7] On the mountain road over Glann the body of an old destitute man was found. Even after the horrific sights that had confronted them in the hovels, the old man's emaciated frame frightened the witnesses.[8] A County Galway priest reported that he met a man with a donkey and cart on which there were three makeshift coffins being transported to the local graveyard. They contained the remains of the man's wife and two children. However, the man was in such a weakened state that he was unable to dig the graves. The following day the priest returned to find to his horror that the corpses were being eaten by ravenous dogs.[9]

These accounts from Glann bear haunting similarities to the horrific scenes witnessed in Skibbereen. In January 1847, Nicholas Cummins, a magistrate from Cork, set out for Skibbereen with a supply of bread to distribute among the poor. He was surprised to find the place almost deserted when he arrived. He entered some of the hovels; in one he was shocked at what lay before him, six famished and ghastly skeletal figures, all apparently dead. They were huddled together in the corner of the room, lying on filthy straw, covered only by a ragged 'horsecloth'. He approached them, and, to his horror, he heard a low moaning sound; they were alive but were suffering from fever. The group consisted of four children, their mother and what had once been their father. Within a short time he was surrounded by at least 200 such phantoms; he had no words to describe these 'frightful spectres' but their 'demonic yells' he could never forget. In another hovel he discovered two corpses 'half-devoured' by rats. Outside another hut he witnessed an emaciated woman in a state of fever, dragging the dead body of her daughter – a girl of about twelve years of age – and attempting to cover her remains with stones.

Another witness encountered an equally heartbreaking experience when he was surrounded by a group of starving people.

He was grabbed from behind, and, upon turning around, he discovered a woman carrying a newly born infant, both of them covered only with a 'filthy sack'.[10]

These accounts from Skibbereen mirror somewhat the accounts witnessed by the Forsters and others from County Galway. Upon arrival in Galway city, the Forsters first visited the workhouse. Again, they were not prepared for what greeted them as they had expected conditions to be better in the capital of Connacht. Having visited the workhouse, William Senior, in a letter to his wife, wrote: 'It was enough to have broken the stoutest heart to have seen the poor little children in the workhouse yesterday – their flesh hanging so loose from their bones, that the physician took it in his hand and wrapped it round their legs.'[11]

They also visited the Claddagh; even this fishing village did not escape the horror, as the famine and contagious diseases knew no boundaries. The Dominican priests had set up a soup kitchen there to help ease the suffering of people who were now in extreme poverty, their numbers diminishing daily from the effects of want. Donations were being requested from outside this independent community to support the Claddagh Cook House.[12]

It was now March, and the weather was still harsh; the benevolent William Forster Junior made a number of observations while being taken around the Claddagh village. There were about 4,000 people living in the Claddagh at the time. They had very little contact with people living in the town except for trading in fish. They married mainly among themselves, and their appointed chief 'was known as the Admiral'; today he is

Famine victims at Kellines, near General Thomson's property.
(*The Illustrated London News*, 1850)

known as king of the Claddagh. As in other areas, the famine had a terrible effect on the people of the Claddagh. Most of their furniture, bedding and clothing had already been sold off to raise finance for food. In one small 'wretched hovel', three emaciated families were found huddled together with only rags to protect themselves from the bitter cold. But even in these terrible conditions, the charity of the Claddagh people shone through. A family there had taken on the burden of looking after a poor blind woman who had no means to support herself.

The question often asked regarding the famine in the Claddagh, and indeed Connemara, is why did the people not eat fish? They lived close to the sea, and many of them were experienced fishermen. A number of theories have been put forward regarding this issue. Some believe that the herring shoals had moved some thirty or forty miles offshore – far out of reach of the small fishing boats.[13] It is evident from a newspaper report in 1847 that the Claddagh fishermen were protecting what fish stocks there were in Galway Bay from fishermen in Salthill, Barna and Oranmore, using force when necessary to prevent the others from fishing.[14]

However, even when the fish shoals were closer to shore many of the Claddagh fishermen did not have the means to fish for them having already pawned their equipment to purchase any available food. The Forsters were obviously aware of this as they went to visit two or three of the largest pawnshops in the town. The proprietors in these pawnshops informed them that they had at least £1,000 worth of such equipment, but the owners did not have the money to redeem their property. It was noted that the pawnshop proprietors were the most prosperous-looking individuals that the Forsters met on their journey. They complained that unless something was done to alleviate the situation they would have to close their businesses as there were no buyers coming into the shops, only people willing to pawn everything they owned, even their clothing.

After this visit, William Forster Junior took the mail train to Dublin where he found similar situations around the capital. He later wrote an account of his experiences and highlighted England's responsibility regarding Ireland. The following is a short extract from the report: 'There is a prevailing idea in England that the newspaper reports are exaggerated. Particular

cases may or may not be coloured; but no colour can deepen
the blackness of the truth; the evil is one which defies all exaggeration.'[15] He felt that England owed it to Ireland to fully support its starving population in return for centuries of neglect
and oppression. The poem below, published in *Tait's Magazine*
and *The Galway Mercury*, was signed J. O'B., Cork, and dated 13
February 1847:

THE FAMINE STRICKEN

You great ones of the earth,
Whose halls each day ring out,
With music and with mirth,
Forget the doom,
That once on Dives fell,
His corpse laid in the tomb,
His soul deep, deep in hell!

And still you dance and sing,
And still your tables groan,
With all that wealth you bring,
From either distance zone,
Your gold and purple doff,
Ere yet it be too late,
Your revellings leave off,
Lo! Famine at your gate.

By yon hovel's cheerless hearth,
Scarce shelter'd from the rain,

Her couch the noisome earth,
A mother writhes in pain,
Around her gauntly spread,
Her ravening offspring cry,
'Bread, bread! dear mother, bread,
Oh! give us, or we die.'

'No bread, my babes! have I.'
The fainting mother cries,
As from her sunken eye,
The scalding tear she dries,
But he who feeds the bird,
Within the tangled wood,
Hath pledged his sacred word,
His children shall have food.

Close to her wasted form,
Her latest-born is prest,
Who draws, still fresh and warm,
The life-stream from her breast,
Two elder children stare,
With wistful eyes yet dim,
As though they longed to share,
That saving draft from him.

Her glazed and sunken eye,
A transient gleam lights up,
She milks her bosom dry,
Then shares the flowing cup,

Thy father went at dawn
Far o'er the mountain side,
And he'll bring his 'Molly Bawn',
Some bread at eventide.

The sun has sunk to rest,
The moon peeps o'er the hill,
The bird has sought her nest,
And all around is still,
Whilst many an anxious eye,
Peers through the thickening gloom,
And many a cear-fraught sigh,
Doth fill that squalid room.

A weary, weary watch,
Long, long may ye maintain,
Nor eye nor ear shall catch,
His form or voice again,
He toil'd the life-long day,
Nor tasted he of bread,
That, when night brought his pay,
The loved ones might be fed.

Slow o'er the dreary heath,
Twelve miles he winds his way,
His tottering limbs beneath,
Refuse their wonted stay,
Oh! that his once-loved hearth,
Again might greet his eyes,

But no; he sinks to earth,
He shivers – grasps – and cries!

The bitter sleet doth pour,
And fiercely howls the blast,
As on that cabin floor,
A mother breaths her last,
All starkly by her lie,
Two forms whence life hath fled,
Oh Christ! that they should die,
In a Christian land for bread.

Oh! stewards of the lord,
Be mindful of your trust,
For the riches which you hoard,
Had turned the ravening tooth,
Of famine from its pray,
And caused the lips of youth,
To bless you night and day.

Then, your gold and purple doff,
Ere yet it be too late,
Your revellings leave off,
Lo! famine's at your gate,
Be mindful of the doom,
That once on Dives fell,
His corpse laid in the tomb,
His soul cast down to hell![16]

7

BLACK FORTY-SEVEN

By May 1847 the town of Galway was densely populated with the influx of unemployed 'half-famished creatures' marching around the streets, carrying flags bearing the slogan 'WE ARE STARVING, BREAD OR EMPLOYMENT'. It was a peaceful protest, but it was only a matter of time before force would come into play in order to secure food. As the famine progressed, desperation set in among the poor, and attacks on food stores and food transports became commonplace. On 7 May 1847 a group of people attacked a consignment of food at Eyre Square, while the same week in the ancient little suburb of Suckeen a group of women attacked a cart and made off with a large sack of flour. Three of the women were later arrested – but the flour had already reached the mouths of the hungry. A large 'mob' assembled at the stores of Henry Comerford and forced the entrance, but they did not do any serious damage and nothing was taken. However, the authorities were becoming concerned and called in the military. A troop of the 7th Hussars and a company of the 49th Regiment were deployed to support the police and continually patrolled the streets to 'protect' the food from the starving.[1]

The population of the town continued to grow with the daily arrival of refugees. It was the same in most of the big towns, and the driving force behind this problem was the absolutely terrible conditions prevailing in the rural areas where people had almost nothing at all to eat. The desperation of these people is evident from the writings of Fr Whyte, a Ballinasloe priest, who, in May 1847 recorded that the health and strength of the youth was similar to that of people in old age – they were all 'withering' before the face of famine. He wept openly at what he witnessed; in one cabin, he administered the last rites to a man whose wife was cooking weeds to try and feed her three children. They had been struck off the famine-relief scheme and were now left to forage for weeds or anything else edible they could find.[2] These were the reasons people sought refuge in the population centres; at least in the towns there was some chance of a meal, either in the workhouse or from one of the benevolent societies. There were also stores of food located in some of the population centres, particularly in port towns, either ready for export or donated foodstuffs arriving from abroad. In addition to this the religious organisations provided some relief. Records show that the Presentation Convent provided some 9,300 meals in January 1847 and 10,300 in February, rising even further over the following months.[3]

One little six-year-old girl, Celia Griffin, walked thirty-five miles from Corindulla, near Ross. She arrived in Galway, along with her family; all of them were in a pitiable condition. She survived for a number of weeks on the streets begging but eventually collapsed from starvation. She was taken to the Presentation Convent where the nuns gave her shelter. Although

Ruins in the village of Carihaken, County Galway.
(*The Illustrated London News*, 1850)

attempts were made to feed her, it was too late for Celia, and within days her little body finally succumbed to starvation. The autopsy report revealed that she had literally died of starvation as there was no trace of food or nourishment in her stomach or digestive system. Celia was just one of thousands of children who died without understanding why.[4]

By May 1847 the town was experiencing some 100 deaths per week from fever and dysentery. The following are some sobering statistics regarding the mortality rates for those years. The death toll in the town for 1847 was 1,919 – a jump of 1,288 from the previous year; this would rise to over 2,000 in 1848. The death toll in the county was 5,556 in 1846, rising to 12,582 in 1847 and reaching a staggering 20,588 by 1849. During 1847 and 1848, over 11,000 inmates died in Galway workhouses. In fact, most of the deaths in the town occurred in the workhouse. While the death rate was extremely high in the workhouse, it was nonetheless still the only refuge for many desperate people.[5] 'Neither wealth, nor rank, nor age, nor sex, escape the ravages of the pestilence,' one newspaper announced.[6]

Mortalities were also recorded among some compassionate landlords who tried to help their tenants and, in doing so, contracted and succumbed to typhus. The following deaths occurring among the gentry were announced in May 1847: J. Nolan, P. Dolphin, S. Jones RM and R. Gregory of Coole Park.[7] When Thomas Martyn of Ballinahinch died; his last words were, 'What will become of my people now?' Marcus Lynch of Renmore House became another victim of the famine when he contracted a fever and died in January 1848.[8]

Doctors who were in the front line of the disaster also paid the price, and by December 1847 eleven of them had died from typhus. Among them were George Seymour of Kilconnel, Charles Donnollon of Annaghdown, Francis Bodkin of Clifden and Edward Lambert of Oranmore. A number of priests from the city and county, two nuns and two agents of the British Relief Association also became victims of fever that year.[9] Among the twelve priests who fell victim to famine-related diseases were Patrick Forde, Parish Priest (PP), Kinvara; Andrew Martyn, PP of Castlegar, Menlo and Carrabrowne; William Hanrahan, Ennistymon; Timothy Geoghegan, PP, Craughwell; Patrick Quinn, PP, Ardrahan; and John Roche, Castlegar. The latter was a brother of Fr B. J. Roche of the parish of St Nicholas in Galway. The newspapers announced that they became martyrs in the heroic performance of their duty. Fr Quinn's body had been discovered at his residence in Labane Lodge after it was noticed he had been missing for a few days.[10]

By June 1847 the authorities in Galway were seriously concerned about the danger of plague breaking out during the summer heat. They announced that the danger arose for the want of a proper burial place for the ever-increasing victims of the famine. It became urgent that additional burial grounds be found as Forthill Cemetery was not sufficient to accommodate the numbers of dead in the town augmented by the influx of destitute starving people.[11] Other cemeteries used included Bushypark, Rahoon, Claddagh and St James, Mervue. Almost all the old cemeteries contain famine burials now long forgotten. Many of them are unmarked except in some cases where a rough stone was pulled from a nearby wall and used to mark the last resting place of a loved one. It also became impossible to provide sufficient coffins for all who were dying. The undertakers solved the problem by supplying a coffin with a false bottom. People still had some degree of dignity and pride, and, to save embarrassment, the corpse was taken to the cemetery in the coffin. Once the coffin was placed in the grave, the false bottom was released, and the body was deposited in the earth. These were mainly shallow graves, covered only with a thin deposit of clay. The coffin was then ready for reuse – over and over again. But these were the 'lucky' ones, as many burials took place with the body covered only in rags or whatever was available and were deposited in a 'famine pit' where hundreds and, indeed, thousands were buried together.[12] The following quote from *The Galway Vindicator* in 1847 refers to these burials:

Cabin of Pat McNamara in the village of Clear.
(*The Illustrated London News*, 1850)

Every where we go, and every quarter of the town, misery stares us in the face. The cries of the poor are still heard. Misery, squalish misery, sickness and death still pervade our streets ... people are suffered to die and be careless buried before our faces, till our very nature has become changed, and cold, and callous – till men, or women, or children are carried to the grave without coffins, on old boards or in sheets, or altogether uncovered.[13]

It was also reported that the only trades which were prospering during this time were the coffin-maker and the grave-digger.[14]

On 19 April 1847, Brother Paul O'Connor wrote to the Galway Relief Committee and informed them that 'starving infants' were now being brought to his Orphans' Breakfast Institute and that the demand for support was increasing daily since the suspension of the public works.[15] He wrote to them again in July of that year and once more warned that the children in his establishment were in great danger of starvation. This was caused by a fall-off in contributions because many of those holding positions of power believed, or at least said they believed, that the new harvest would end the catastrophe; this attitude proved fatal for the starving people. Brother O'Connor also stated that the situation remained very serious even if there was a good harvest and added, 'But alas for our poor Orphans – though the ground had been watered by sweat from their fathers' brow and by their mothers' tears, this sweat was only absorbed in the grave.'[16] He was extremely concerned that the children would follow their parents to the famine pit. His appeal was heartbreaking:

> Sickly and emaciated as many of the poor children are at present, their condition will, I fear, be much worse when the 'ration system' ceases on the 15th of August; and if some means be not provided, in time, to meet that emergency, I am seriously apprehensive – from what I know, by long experience of the habitual wretchedness – that the 16th of August will be, to them, the beginning of a second famine as fatal as the first, even though the harvest should realise our fondest hopes and the granaries of the farmer be filled to overflowing.[17]

O'Connor was a tireless worker for these children, and this is just one of many letters of appeal that he wrote to the authorities and the newspapers during the famine years. While he seems to have believed that the potato crops would yield a good harvest, he also warned that conditions would be even more horrific if there was another bad harvest. According to his letter, there were 500 children in the Orphans' Breakfast Institute, and they were averaging between 2,700 and 2,800 breakfasts per week. His concerns were well founded, and the appalling situation continued to deteriorate as the year wore on.[18] Many of the children being fed were from the Claddagh, and it must have brought him some relief when, on 1 August 1847, the Claddagh Piscatory School was officially opened. The purpose of the school was to provide a practical education for the Claddagh children; the boys were taught the art of net-making and girls were trained in lace work.[19] It was a serious attempt to try to give the children the necessary skills that would help them become more self-sufficient and enterprising.

One of the main people involved in the foundation of the school was Fr Thomas Rushe of the Dominican Order.[20] Fr Rushe had travelled throughout Ireland and England collecting funds for the erection of the school; he also secured a grant from the Commissioners of National Schools.[21] In its first year, £66 was also raised to support the efforts of the teachers. The venture proved successful, and by 1850 over 500 pupils had been educated in the school.[22] The building of the school also provided employment in a deprived area, as did the building of the model school, which was opened by 1850 on the Newcastle Road. It was located quite close to the workhouse.[23]

In the small parish of Bohermore, on the outskirts of the old town of Galway, at least five people per day perished. Fr Roche,

PP, told the relief committee, which was now meeting daily, that his parishioners were trying to survive on nettles and other wild plants.[24] The abject poverty in the parish was appalling; 5,000 were signing on for relief. Fr Roche had attended 130 sick calls in the previous weeks, and in one house alone he had to anoint four members of the same family. The dreaded dysentery that had broken out was taking its toll in sickness and in lives. In many cases there was no person available to give those in fever a drink of cold water to ease their suffering. Tradition tells us that in a field located just outside Menlo village, overlooking Lough Corrib, people dying of fever were laid out so their bodies would be cooled by the breeze from the lake, giving some relief from suffering before death finally took them. The field was known locally as the *gort na marbhe* – the field of the dead.

The priests at the forefront of the disaster complained bitterly to the authorities and to their superiors about the conditions that faced them daily. Bishop O'Donnell of Galway called on the government to provide a permanent solution to the problem; he also called for the 'Repeal of the Union' and appealed to people to purchase only goods produced in Ireland.[25] In July 1847 he became concerned, as did everyone else, when it was reported that the workhouse in Newcastle was to close. The authorities were warned that if the workhouse closed then the deplorable situation in Galway would multiply. Eventually funds were made available to keep the workhouse open.[26]

Also in July, people in Philadelphia were raising money for relief in Galway. Thomas Folan of Dominick Street was their local contact, and he informed the Galway town commissioners of the news. Flour, cornmeal, rye flour and other foodstuffs were transported to Galway on the brig *Islam* under the command of Captain James Lofland. It was the first aid that Galway had received from the USA, and it was extremely welcome; in fact, as the weeks passed, an hourly vigil was kept at Galway docks by the local authorities and, of course, the starving. When the ship finally arrived, Captain Lofland was welcomed as a hero by all concerned.[27] The bells of St Nicholas church rang out in joy and thanksgiving for the life-saving food from Philadelphia. In addition to this, a former Galway businessman, Dudley Persse, who was living in New York, sent a ship loaded with 4,000 barrels of foodstuffs for the relief of his native city.[28]

Other shipments of food and clothing arrived in Galway in August. There were four shipments between July and August, organised by Irish people in the USA and the Quakers. This support, along with local donations, relieved the food shortages in Galway city temporarily.[29] However, there were worse days ahead, and desperation forced people to risk all to stay alive. In October, two carts of flour were 'plundered' near Renmore House, the residence of P. M. Lynch. Some of the people responsible were later caught, but the flour was never recovered.[30] By the end of 1847, seventy-three people had been sentenced to transportation from Galway city and county for stealing food supplies.[31] The local authorities were dreading the oncoming winter and reported that the government was doing little to alleviate the problem.[32]

News from around the county in October 1847 was extremely gloomy. A coastguard officer recorded that two-thirds of the population in Connemara was destitute. He stated that many of the ratepayers had also become paupers and yet collectors, aided by police, were out daily, seizing apparel and tools. Death from exposure loomed for those evicted from their humble dwellings. In many areas, the homes of those evicted were levelled to prevent them from returning. The tenants salvaged sections of their rooftops and placed them over ditches to provide shelter from the terrible winter conditions. One priest writing from Clifden said, 'How I wish the real suffering of the people could reach the ears of the rich of this life … The destitute starve in one world, while the landowning classes inhabit another.'[33] Fr Thomas Walsh from Rosmuc stated that his parishioners were like spectres without hair as a result of fever and had little clothing to protect themselves from this 'awful weather'.

Galway city was again being 'swamped' by evicted paupers from Connemara.[34] By November 1847, the workhouse was packed, and additional staff had to be employed to try to cope with the situation. It was pointed out that the chaplain, Fr Daly, also required curates as he could not sufficiently attend to the spiritual needs of upwards of 1,000 inmates, most of whom were fever-stricken. It was reported that all the priests who attended the sick had also caught the fever – in fact some of them twice. Those unable to gain admission to the workhouse 'thronged the doors of the townspeople, demanding a morsel of food'.[35] It is little wonder that so many people were continuing to arrive in the town given the sheer scale of evictions and the circumstances faced when evicted, as can be seen from the following two reports. The first appeared in *The Galway Mercury* in October 1847 and the second in *The Galway Vindicator* in December that same year.

(1) EXTERMINATION: THE COURT OF CHANCERY

On Thursday last John M. O'Hara, Esq. Deputy Sheriff, accompanied by a large party of police and posse of bailiffs, attended on the lands of Cloonaglasha, to take possession under a civil bill ejectment decree, of several unfortunate wretches, tenants of Bishop Daly. Mr O'Hara subsequently proceeded to the village of Slievard, part of the Belmount property, over which a receiver of the Court of Chancery has been extended for several years past in the cause of Martin against Blake, and dispossessed eighteen families, whose houses were levelled to the ground, leaving over 100 unfortunate human beings without a place of shelter, on the approach of the bleak winter's blast. May God help the poor creatures, victims of a system which punishes misfortune with greater vigour than crime. It appears from our informant, that James Cuff Blake made a joint lease of the lands to those poor people, and received their rack rent, or a very considerable portion of it, in labour; after his death a large arrear accumulated, either through negligence of the former receiver, or the inability of his tenants to pay, the solvent industrious man being under the joint tenancy system, libel for the rent of those who died, or neglected their portions. We know the present receiver Mr James Blake Concannon to be a most humane, kind-hearted man, but he had no direction in the case, the consequence of which is the melancholy extermination of a whole village.[36]

(2) FRIGHTFUL INFLUX OF EVICTED COTTIER PAUPERS

For the past week the town has been literally inundated with a tide of rural pauperism well calculated to affright the public, and excite even the most torpid and liveliest feelings of commiseration towards the unfortunate creatures themselves, and the warmest indignation towards their ruthless exterminators. The streets are swarming with these wretched outcasts of landlord despotism, who, unable to procure admission to the Workhouse, throng the doors of the inhabitants demanding a morsel of food to save them from perishing. We indulge in no exaggeration.[37]

In October 1847, two ships, the *Islam* and *Saone*, arrived in Galway port from the USA with a consignment of flour, meal and clothes from the Society of Friends. The society in Galway stored the clothes and sold the flour to try to raise funds to buy larger quantities of food for distribution later in the year, closer to Christmas, when they believed that the situation would be a great deal worse. They also sent some of the supplies to Limerick, and, because of this, they received much criticism.[38]

Just when the authorities believed that the situation could not get any worse, as Christmas approached, eleven large boatloads of homeless people from islands off the west coast arrived at Galway quay, all of them seeking assistance, thus adding greatly to the already deteriorating problem. In contrast to this deplorable situation, 'Superior Smoked Hams' were being advertised in some newspapers for Christmas, indicating that there was wealth among some of the townspeople.[39] By the end of 1847, Galway and, indeed, Ireland had changed, changed forever; that year had

An eviction scene in Connacht. (*The Illustrated London News*, 1870)

certainly earned its infamous name, 'Black Forty-Seven'. The following poem was written by C. MacSweeney and published in *The Galway Mercury* in 1847. It depicts the absolute horrors of that year:

A LAY OF SORROW

Ochone! I' ne'er must smile again,
Dark night has settled on my breast,
My people lie around me slain,
By fate and foes at once opprest!

They die, great God, how fast they die,
In their cold cabins all alone,
No wake – no mass – no funeral cry,
Festering by their hearths ochone!

Along that way I see them bear,
All rudely on a truckle thrown,
The corpses of an aged pair,
In youth I knew them well, ochone!

That woman nursed me, when a child –
A kind and hearty nurse was she,
He told me tales of prowess wild,
Of Finn and Fenian chivalry.

There on a door they bear a mother,
Clasped to her breast her youngest born,
Beside her, weeping, limps another –
The father has been dead since morn.

We turn for mercy to thy face,
Lord, shed it largely from thy throne,

For we have been a faithful race,
Faithful even to death, ochone!

O Christ, when wilt thou send relief,
Where hath thy loving-kindness flown?
Oh, we have enough of grief,
Now let our sorrow end, ochone![40]

8

ANOTHER YEAR OF SADNESS

By January 1848, the situation in Galway was becoming more and more alarming as the horrors of famine had already sent so many people to an early grave. The workhouse was unable to cope with the sheer mass of destitute and starving arriving at its doors everyday seeking aid. It was reported that 'Not a day passes that does not behold the condition of the town becoming increasingly alarming. Famine with all its horrors is rapidly making its way amongst us, and its "comitant" death, has already snatched away hundreds to the grave.'[1] There were at least 3,000 starving people with scarcely a rag to cover them roaming the streets. On the bitter cold morning of 26 January 1848, two children were found naked and dead in High Street, while another child was found in the same condition in an adjacent street; all three had succumbed to starvation and exposure. The hospitals, poorhouses and even the jail were full. The city and county jail was built to accommodate fewer than 200 prisoners but at this time was trying to house some 900 inmates and fifty children. The clergy were also overcome with the task of attending to the sick and dying, among them the jail inmates.[2]

As with the previous year, 1848 also saw serious concern among the local authorities because of the additional burials in Forthill Cemetery. Many of these victims were inmates of Galway Jail. Such was the death rate in the town that the authorities were left with no alternative; they had to stop the burials coming from the jail. Notice of their decision was given to the governor of the jail. In April, the Inspector General of Prisons was sent to Galway by the government to investigate the situation. When he had assessed the state of affairs, it was decided that burial 'accommodation' would need to be identified for the 'multitudes of unfortunate prisoners, who are daily hurried to the grave'.[3]

There was also a fear that more pressure would be placed on the prison management because the Galway Union had issued a public warning to 'paupers' who were begging and receiving rations from the authorities at the same time. If they were caught begging their names would be immediately removed from the list of people in need of rations. They could not receive food from any area except the district in which they resided. A list of paupers was also issued to the police, and anyone arrested for vagrancy would be questioned by the relieving officer of the district to determine why they had left their own area.[4] The people who failed to gain relief or who lost their support really had only two choices: to commit a crime and end up in jail or to seek admission to the workhouse. Conditions in both places were far from satisfactory, but it was better than lying down in the street to die.

There are many accounts of people dying while attempting the journey to the workhouse, as with Mary Commons, the woman who died on the Dangan road. Another victim who suffered the same fate was Mark Murphy from Spiddal. He was in such an emaciated state when he attempted to walk to the workhouse in January 1848 that death overcame him on the road near Barna. He was just another 'victim to the ruthless policy of our present rulers', the report declared.[5] Under the heading 'More Deaths by Starvation', a reporter from *The Galway Mercury* indicated that the death toll was so enormous in the villages located just outside the city that conditions could only be compared with Schull or Skibbereen, which were amongst the worst hit areas during the famine.

> Were we to enumerate in detail the deaths which daily take place in this and the neighbouring localities, from STARVATION, our columns could not be sufficient to contain the sad and melancholy record. On all sides we see the work of devastation going on, and hundreds hurried into eternity by the grim monster – FAMINE …

At Gormuna, Connemara – the embers of life. (*The Graphic*, 1880)

If we turn to Oranmore we are forced to witness the greater part of the population in a state of the most abject misery that can be imagined. The people there are falling victims, not by units but by hundreds. Their pastors, unable to bear the accumulated load of wretchedness, have themselves become tenants of the tomb – and almost all who are left seem more like spectres from another world than inhabitants of this. Equal in point of suffering, to Skull [*sic*] or Skibbereen, Oranmore presents to the philanthropist the opportunity of exercising his charitable disposition and of rescuing many a human being from starvation. May we hope that should this come under the notice of any one to whom the Lord has entrusted the Stewardship of this world's wealth, he shall not be unmindful of the wretched creatures who pine away from utter destitution in this doomed locality.[6]

The following is from an eyewitness account of visitors to Skibbereen and Schull. James Mahoney, an artist from Cork, and a companion witnessed some terrible scenes at Chapel Yard in Skibbereen. They discovered that six members of the Barrett family had been evicted, struggled to this old burial ground and literally entombed themselves in a small watch-house, seven feet by six feet wide. At the doorway lay the bodies of two or three children; in fact, this hut was surrounded by a 'rampart of human bones ... In this horrible den, in the midst of a mass of human putrefaction, six individuals, males and females, labouring under the most malignant fever, were huddled together, as closely as were the dead in the graves around.'[7] Later that night they returned with bread, tea and sugar, and although it was blowing a gale at the time, the groans of the people in the watch-house could be heard above the wind and rain. As Mahoney was about to enter, he immediately had to draw back, such was the intolerable 'effluvium'. He was completely unnerved at the horrific scene of suffering and misery. All these people requested was a drink of water. The family were removed to a fever hospital the following day.

During their journey, Mahoney and his companion had another pitiful and 'memorable' request for water; this was at the home of a man named Tim Harrington. Four people had lain dead for six days in his hut, killed by the fever, and, as he made his way to the door, he collapsed. Tragically, they were unable to give the man any assistance, as they feared contracting the disease themselves. In Schull they encountered some 300 women trying to buy food. Some of them had queued from daybreak to purchase Indian meal from government-appointed officers,

Landing Indian meal at Inishboffin Island.
(*The Illustrated London News*, 1886)

who were issuing 'miserable quantities' at high 'famine prices'.[8] Another visitor to the town remarked that some of the children in Schull looked like 'decrepit old women, their faces wrinkled, their bodies bent and distorted with pain, their eyes looking like those of a corpse'.[9]

Despite all the deaths over the previous years, evictions continued. In March 1848, on the 'bleak seashore' of Galway, several tenant families were forced out of their homes in terrible weather conditions. Their pleas for permission to stay at least overnight were refused. It was reported that some of the people died, among them children, 'not from want, but from this wanton and brutal exposure'.[10] A family named Shanahan – father, mother and five children – who lived in Menlough, County Galway, were all found dead in their little cabin. Although they were facing starvation, the father had paid the rent to his landlord a number of days previously, and, with no relief forthcoming, the entire family died.[11] In July, Fr James Dwyer, the parish priest in Lackagh near Claregalway, witnessed those evicted dying on the roadside, under bridges and in sheds. He frequently had to crawl on his knees into these 'abodes of death' to visit his parishioners before they succumbed to their fate.[12]

Troops were deployed to aid with evictions around the county; one report in June 1848 stated that a troop of 'Scots Greys' were sent out from Loughrea to oversee the demolition of ten houses at Grange. The tenants' only option was to make their way to the poorhouse.[13] In the neighbouring County Mayo, horse and foot soldiers, and a group of 'well-paid' men, arrived in Ballinrobe to evict forty-eight starving families from their homes. The fact that it was at Christmas made no difference to the landlord; they were simply turned out onto the road. These people could not gain admittance to the workhouse and were left wandering on the roads.[14] Some people who were evicted in neighbouring counties eventually made their way to Galway, but many died on this 'trail of tears'. Following a visit to the west of Ireland, the Inspector of Roads reported that he had to bury 140 corpses he found on his way to Clifden.

Picking up a meal upon the coast, Killary Bay. (*The Graphic*, 1880)

People in the Annaghdown district, some ten miles from Galway city, were so debilitated and deaths were so numerous that corpses could not be taken to the churchyard. Local tradition indicates that every field in that area contains the remains of famine victims. At least two mass famine pits were dug near Tuam such were the fatalities in this area.[15] As one can see from the numerous reports, many of those who died were essentially victims of eviction. Under the heading 'More Evictions', in July 1848, *The Galway Vindicator* reported the destruction of an entire village and its people being forced onto the road:

> A few days ago the sheriff of the county paid a visit to the lands of Gurrane, in the neighbourhood of Athenry, on the estate of a man calling himself the Honourable Col Bermingham Sewell, and demolished the entire village of Cahertubber, leaving but two houses standing, one of which was converted into a depot for the remnant of roofing of those that were not committed to the flames. The wretched and unhappy victims are to be found squatted upon the road side, presenting the most frightful appearance of destitution. In vain have those beings looked for compassion from the Honourable Col, although all their gardens are well cropped, and a few short weeks of bounteous Providence would have left them in a situation to discharge the trifling demands of this most Christian landlord, whose liberality, generosity, and hospitality are in perfect keeping with his honourable cognomen.[16]

In Galway, things looked a little brighter when work on the Eglinton Canal began on 8 March 1848, at an estimated cost of £27,000. This development would give controlled access from the lakes to the sea and also gave additional employment at a vital time for the authorities. The work included the building of five bascule bridges across the canal. These bridges could be drawn to one side to allow barges and boats to pass through. Two lock houses were also constructed, one at Cong and the other at Ball's Bridge, Dominick Street, Galway.[17] The work took just over four years, providing secure employment for many during that time. The Earl of Eglinton, the Lord Lieutenant of Ireland, opened the canal on 20 August 1852. Thousands turned out to see the steamer *O'Connell*, carrying the vice-regal party, make its way through the canal. There was much excitement, and an air of optimism was beginning to slip back into the townspeople.[18]

However, this was not the case in 1848; while employment looked optimistic, rumours of a new potato blight began to circulate again, causing much concern. While the potato crop of 1847 had been successful, it was not enough to end the hardship and hunger. The reason for this was simple – not enough potatoes had been planted owing to the high cost of seed. People were determined not to let the same thing happen in 1848. Those who could afford the cost of the seeds purchased as much as possible. Others sold off whatever livestock they had and did the same. The people still had trust in the potato and were reluctant to sow other crops; thousands of lives were now dependent on the risk everyone was taking. Tragically, the entire crop failed that year, forcing thousands more to seek aid from the already overburdened relief system.[19] The oncoming winter looked bleaker than ever, and, as December 1848 arrived, more poverty-stricken people made their way to the town. None gained admittance to the workhouses as they were already overcrowded. *The Galway Vindicator* stated that from 'early morning to dead of night' the town experienced harrowing scenes of suffering not seen in any other district, with droves of men, women and children, scarcely covered in rags, weeping and wailing and, as in the previous year, knocking at the doors of the inhabitants begging for a morsel of food to stay alive. The process repeated itself over and over again until another year of sadness closed.[20]

Arrival of gun-boat *Banterer* at Inishboffin with meal for the starving inhabitants. (*The Illustrated London News*, 1886)

The following poem was composed for *The University Magazine* and was published in *The Galway Mercury*. It is a poignant acknowledgement of the evicted peasants:

LAMENT OF THE EJECTED IRISH PEASANT

The night was dark and dreary; Agra gal machree.
And the heart that loves you weary; Agra gal machree.
For every hope is blighted,
That bloomed when first we plighted,
Our troth, and were united; Agra gal machree.

We had once a happy hearth; Agra gal machree.
None happier on earth; Agra gal machree.
Thy love smile made it so,
And toil caused our store's o'er flow,
Leaving something to bestow; Agra gal machree.

Oft when the biting blast; Agra gal machree.
Sent the stranger shivering past; Agra gal machree.
Would thy beaming eye flow o'er,
As thy hand flung wide the door,
To bid welcome to the poor; Agra gal machree.

Still our homestead we behold; Agra gal machree.
But the cheerful hearth is cold; Agra gal machree.
And those around its glow,
Assembled long ago,
In the cold, cold earth lie low; Agra gal machree.

Twas famine's wasting breath; Agra gal machree.
That winged the shaft of death; Agra gal machree.
And the landlord lost to feeling,

Who drove us from our sheeling,
Though we prayed for mercy kneeling; Agra gal machree.

Oh! twas heartless from that floor; Agra gal machree.
Where our fathers dwelt of yore; Agra gal machree.
To fling our offspring – seven,
Neath the winter skies of heaven,
To perish on that even; Agra gal machree.

But the sleeping blast blows chill; Agra gal machree.
Let me pass thee closer still; Agra gal machree.
To this scratched bleeding heart,
For too soon – too soon we part; Agra gal machree.

Oh! there's a God above; Agra gal machree.
Of mercy and of love; Agra gal machree.
May he look down this night,
From his heavenly throne of light,
On our sad forlorn plight; Agra gal machree.[21]

9

WILL HUNGER EVER END?

On 9 February 1849, the Cabinet Secretary, Charles Greville, recorded in his diary that Irish people were dying of hunger and the government did not know what to do. There was no actual plan to combat the disaster, and, to make matters worse, there was 'nothing but disagreement' among the ministers and only paralysis and hard-heartedness presided. However, there were others who believed that something could be done, at least in the coastal regions. By 1849, many contemporaries believed that the neglect of the Irish fishing industry by the government was the cause of starvation in these areas. Given that Ireland was surrounded by ocean, some local authorities believed that if this natural resource was exploited to its full advantage and managed properly, the fishing industry could employ up to 100,000 people. This, they believed, had the capability of feeding 1 million people. The local authorities stated that the seas around Ireland were teeming with fish and the government still continued to waste finance in areas that would have no economic return, thus ignoring the most important resource available to them. Some complained about the amounts of money that had been expended on building roads, some of which were of no importance and were not required, simply to employ people. Many of the roads were left in an unfinished and dangerous state.

The Irish Fishing Board had been dissolved in 1830, which resulted in a continuous decline of the industry. This decision left fishermen unaided and, as a result, they were just about able to make a living from the sea; there was no finance available to invest in boats capable of deep-sea fishing. The situation was not helped by the fact that in 1847 the Protestant Archbishop of Dublin, Richard Whately, told the House of Lords that a clerical friend had informed him that if finance were advanced to the fishermen in Queenstown (Cobh), County Cork, rather than have their boats equipped properly they would spend it all on food. However, this statement was challenged by members of the Society of Friends, who pointed out that after William Forster had visited Galway he secured £100 for the Claddagh fishermen, which resulted in sixty-eight boats being put to sea and a rich harvest amounting to £800 worth of fish caught in one month alone. This was a major contribution in the fight against starvation in the village. At least hunger was kept at bay; disease was a different matter that had to be dealt with separately. The Archbishop was criticised for believing the 'imagination' of one cleric with regard to the Cork fishermen. He was also accused of insinuating that the Irish were lazy, which did not help the situation in Ireland. The question asked was, 'had he not witnessed' the poverty-stricken men begging for work on relief schemes in every part of the country, men who could scarcely walk from want, some even dying while trying to earn a wage to feed their families?[1] This put an end to these accusa-

The general state of affairs, Galway.
(*The Illustrated London News*, 1880)

tions, but it did not really help the fishermen, and the finance required to revive the Irish fishing industry to its full potential was not made available.

The Quakers continued to support the Claddagh fishermen, and in 1849 they made trawling equipment available so they could fish in deeper waters. However, there was reluctance at first amongst the fishermen to trawl in deeper waters as they wanted to fish using their own traditional methods.[2] It was believed by these fishermen that if they fished the waters before a certain day, or fished every consecutive night, the fish would move to safer waters. This belief came to a rapid end when they discovered that boats from County Clare were fishing in the bay 'without permission from the Claddagh High Admiral', and, to make matters worse, their catch was being sold at the Galway market.[3] These circumstances overcame the prejudices and superstitions, and the Claddagh fishermen were soon reclaiming their old fishing grounds. The 'Claddagh Curing House' opened and advertised that it was in a position to supply smoked and pickled herrings, dried and pickled hake, whiting and pollack.[4] While the fishing was successful, they were only getting 'half price' for the fish. They complained bitterly that people were taking full advantage of them because they did not have any tillage to 'fall back on', which resulted in their being forced to sell their hard-earned produce at a substantially lower price than pre-famine prices.[5] The situation deteriorated, and hopes of fewer deaths in 1849 were soon dashed as the Claddagh suffered a huge outbreak of cholera, which made no distinction between young or old. There were so many children dying that it proved impossible to record all of their names. The cemetery books simply recorded the number of children who died on a particular day or week. A pandemic of cholera spread across Europe that year and caused the deaths of 600 in Galway town and a further 4,000 in the county.[6] One of the early cholera victims in the Claddagh was the esteemed 'Admiral'. He died in April 1849. His death was reported on 28 April 1849 in *The Galway Vindicator*, under the heading, 'Death of the Admiral of the Claddagh Fishermen'. As can be seen from the following letter, his brother succumbed to the same disease:

> The fine, honest, old fisherman, 'Bartley Hynes' who, according to one of their aboriginal customs, was elected in August '46 Admiral or King of the simple, singular people of the Claddagh, died on Thursday last, from an attack of cholera. He was we believe, the first amongst them seized by the fatal disease, and nothing could equal their consternation but their grief at his dangerous illness.

The place resounded with their lamentations, and they crowded round him notwithstanding their intense dread of contagion. Indeed if all monarchs were so beloved by their subjects as poor Bartley, we should have had few revolutions. On the other hand, the Admiral bore himself in a manner worthy of his high title. With complete self-possession he prepared for death, having Rev. Mr Commins, and Rev. Mr Folan present, and even continued to direct the efforts made to alleviate the disease, affirming coolly and positively to nearly the last moment, that if ever a man got through it he would – speaking of it metaphorically as if he were weathering out a storm. His life's voyage, poor fellow, was however soon at an end, despite his intrepidity. It is a singular fact that his brother was also seized by cholera at Kinvara, and died about the same time. The messenger who came across the bay, to inform him of his brother's death found the Admiral dead also.[7]

While the support from the Quakers was welcome and regular, the devastation of the Claddagh fishing industry is very apparent when one considers that before 1845 it was reported that there were some '3000 stalwart fishermen' making a living from the sea. In the years following the famine the situation remained critical, and within twenty years the fishing-crew population was reduced to just over 200, which was a major cause of poverty in the area. It was said that many of these people were spending half their lives in and out of the workhouse. A fortnight's scarcity of fish or bad weather had a terrible effect on the community as most of them had little or nothing to fall back on for support. This resulted in equipment again ending up in the pawnshops. Most of the able-bodied men emigrated to the USA. By the end of the nineteenth century, the situation had improved somewhat as the remaining fishermen managed to utilise other commodities from the sea, such as seaweed, and landed it in large quantities. It was then sold to the factories where it was used in the production of iodine and various other products.[8]

The Claddagh, Galway. (*The Illustrated London News*, 1880)

Throughout all of the suffering during the famine years an abundance of food for export was continually arriving in the town. This is evident from the final section of a report by the Catholic curate of St Nicholas', M. A. Kavanagh. In February 1849 he wrote of the appalling living conditions of the people in Bohermore. He said that he visited five 'sick cases' in that locality on a wet and windy day. Upon entering the first house he found himself standing in a pool of water as the roof was leaking badly and was damaged in a number of places. It was very cold, and there was a constant 'dull-sounding splash' as rainwater from the roof dripped into the pool. He called out to see if there was anyone still in the house. At first there was no reply, but a short time later a woman of about thirty years of age appeared from another room, holding a 'wailing infant' in her arms. Upon seeing the priest, she begged, 'Mercy for my children and me; we are starving. We have eaten nothing for two days. Give us something.' The young woman was half naked, covered only in a 'filthy' inner garment. The curate, thinking that he was in the wrong house, explained that he was not out to visit her and asked her where the Devany family lived. 'They are here,' she replied, and again pleaded for assistance for herself and her child. At that moment, Mr Devany's daughter entered the room; she had been out to beg for a candle to light for him when he arrived. When she lit the candle in the inner room, the light revealed two 'living skeletons'. They were her father and mother lying on beds of straw on the 'watery floor in different corners' of the room. There was no fire, no furniture, not so much as a utensil; it was difficult to believe that this man had once been a 'well-to-do' tradesman.

After giving the Devanys the last rites, Fr Kavanagh made his second sick call; this was to a family living just up the street from the Devany household. He reported that this cabin was of the meanest sort; its room was scarcely sufficient to stable an ass. He found the woman whom he was called out to visit huddled in a corner of the room; she was very ill. In another room he discovered her two daughters; the younger girl was shivering and weeping. Their father was seated on a low stool between them. He was crouching over a single coal of fire, his face had every expression of want and forlorn hope in it. His son was out trying to collect some cabbage leaves. They had had nothing to eat for three days, and having completed his duties in this humble abode Fr Kavanagh moved on. His next two calls were to the Caulfield families, and he found them in similar living and physical conditions. His last call was to the Dowd family, and he found these people living in even worse circumstances than any of the others. He simply reported:

> I fear to describe the misery I saw here. It is enough to say that he [the father] died on the following day. I am sure before Heaven! he died of pure and absolute starvation … He was buried in the deep darkness of a wet and stormy night. And still – what a thought for the world! Our town was never, never fuller of corn and flour and meal![9]

It was all awaiting export.

Similar reports began arriving from Mayo that same month when the rector in Westport stated in an extended letter that 'at this moment there are hundreds of individuals dying about me of actual starvation, although we have a poor law!'[10] He also reported that he visited the home of a woman who had given birth to a baby while in a terrible fever. Her mother, father and husband were already dead of disease in the cabin. The situation was so brutal that the death of neighbours became meaningless. A widow, 'a most respectable lady', with seven children, all on the 'brink of the grave' from starvation arrived seeking aid, but there was none available. 'The wants of my poor Roman Catholic parishioners are extreme; they are

The Fish Market, Galway. (*The Illustrated London News*, 1880)

dying in numbers daily and hourly from starvation.'[11] Upon visiting the cabins, he often found two and three famished people in one 'bed' trying to keep warm, such were the winter conditions. He stated that parents were actually thanking God for taking away their famine-stricken children, who had died of hunger and cold.

Some of those strong enough were walking from Louisburg to Westport in the hope of gaining support, or at least access to the workhouse. People from all over Mayo were converging on Westport, as it was the main port for that county. The huge granaries located along the Westport quay were well stocked with grain while these poverty-stricken people were making their way to be transported to the emigration ships waiting just outside the harbour.

The people involved in relief work continued to petition at every opportunity, writing and lobbying in every way that they could. A letter addressed to Lord John Russell, and also published in the newspapers in March 1849, made it abundantly clear that the situation in Ireland was still extremely critical. The Protestant rector of Louisburg, County Mayo, wrote it:

> The wants of my parishioners are extreme, dying in numbers daily from starvation, and in the annals of the world never was heard of such patience under such unparalleled sufferings – Frequently I have known of two of a family lying dead in one cabin from starvation, and it causes not the least excitement in my locality. The recipients of outdoor relief are starving three days in the week. The sandbanks around me are studded with bodies of the dead – the very graves in my churchyard have, in my presence, been assailed by starving dogs ... The beasts in the field, the hog in the sty are infinitely better provided for. If the worst criminal in the land were condemned to starve upon such terms his fate would excite compassion and command attention, whilst the fate of thousands, innocent and unoffending, is viewed with heartlessness and without remonstrance.[12]

On St Patrick's Day 1849 the workhouse union announced that twenty-five deaths had taken place that week. One hundred and eighty-six people had been admitted, pushing the total workhouse population in Galway city to 3,310. In addition to this, the union was also trying to provide some outdoor relief.[13] One woman who had collected the rations for her family at the workhouse absconded, leaving her husband to starve. The man attempted to find her and 'died from want' on the road leading into the town. The same day, a child of about two years of age was found in an emaciated state in one of the lanes of the town and died later that night. The parents of the child could not be located. In another instance, the body of a man named Cloonan was found at the gate of Ballyduggan estate.[14]

The suffering caused both physical and mental agony for everyone; the question asked many times was 'Will hunger ever end?' It would – when everyone was dead! The situation was worsening; there were even reports of alleged cannibalism coming from Clifden, which stated that a mother whose children had died had eaten part of one child's leg.[15] The reporters may have been misinformed, but it does pose the question of whether this was an isolated occurrence.[16] Even in Galway the death rate among children was higher than one could imagine. The following extract from another letter of appeal from Brother Paul O'Connor to the authorities in March 1849 indicates why so many children died:

The other day, for instance, a poor boy seeking some relief observed, in the passage leading to the Schools, a few scattered grains of Indian meal that had accidentally fallen there a day or two before, and finding that the particles were so detached and small as to elude the grasp of his fingers he made sure and short work of the novel repast by placing himself on his hands and knees, and in that posture lapped up with his tongue the tempting dust from the pavement. Another scene of more recent date, and of a more shocking nature, I have, with others, witnessed within this very week, and the like of which I had never heard of. It was simply this. A fellow-creature – ho yes! one with an immortal soul made in God's own image, redeemed by the Saviour's blood and destined for a throne in Heaven – a fellow-creature metamorphosed into a moving skeleton and only half-covered with rags, trying to extract nutriment from the marrow-less cavity of a bone that had been previously gnawed by a hungry dog, and that had been blanched by sun and rain for several days. I should never have done were I to fully describe the sufferings of the poor children from sickness, cold and hunger. At the very moment which I write these lines (Friday morning) the ground is covered with snow; and behold! there they come in crowds, shivering and shoeless and crying, and half-dead with cold coming to their poor daily meal. Oh God help them! What will they do? What will become of them when even that one meal shall have failed them?[17]

An eviction scene, County Mayo. (*The Illustrated London News*, 1886)

Galway jail had, over the famine years, accommodated thousands of people who were found guilty of petty crime. However, by 1849 it was unable to cope with the high numbers still being sent there. Some people were even resorting to breaking windows in the police barracks around the city and county to ensure a prison sentence. There seemed to be no end to the influx of homeless and hungry people arriving in the town; they were even coming from the neighbouring counties, thus adding to the crime problems. Complaints were made to magistrates about their practice of having paupers charged with vagrancy sent to jail and many of them were released 'into the town' a few hours later. It was a serious worry for the authorities, and it was felt that it should be brought to the attention of the Lord Lieutenant, as should the 'shocking state' of the prison. The authorities wanted the situation emphasised to him in a 'most forceful' manner.

An urgent demand was also made for the legislature to amend the vagrancy act. They suggested that a place of confinement should be constructed adjacent to the workhouse for vagrants rather than having them committed to prison.[18] Some prisoners were also being transferred from smaller towns around County Galway, such as from the Bridewell in Oughterard, where prisoners were marched to Galway in torrential rain, adding to their misery.[19] One observer in Galway jail reported that 'the ravages of destitution are upon almost every face – a spectator can feel their condition but never describe it.'[20]

During an inquest into the deaths of two prisoners, Thomas Kyne and Patt Conneely, the governor of the town prison, Abraham Marshall, gave a descriptive account of the conditions prevailing within the prison walls. He said that when the prisoners were placed in his custody they were already in a 'sickly emaciated state' and greatly reduced by 'want'. He informed the inquest that the prison was totally overcrowded, with five or six times more prisoners incarcerated than it had been built to accommodate. There were thirty-six rooms measuring seven feet high and five feet wide, where four people were forced to sleep. There were ten other rooms measuring fifteen feet by six feet where twelve prisoners were being accommodated. A large number of prisoners were sleeping in the passages and lobbies, with only straw for a bed and without a covering of any kind. The only protection they had from the cold was the 'filthy rags' that they wore. The day room which the prisoners were forced to occupy during wet weather measured twenty feet long by twelve feet wide. As many as seventy-four prisoners frequented the day room at any given time, leaving no escape from health hazards. The prison hospital was also overcrowded, making conditions even worse.

As brutal as conditions were in the prison, Marshall stated that if the gates were to be opened the prisoners would have to be forced to leave. He also said that some prisoners were brought to the jail in carts and were so weak from exhaustion and hunger that they could not even crawl into the prison without assistance. Many of them were already close to death when they arrived. In the case of Thomas Kyne and Patt Conneely, they were incarcerated for petty crimes committed out of total desperation. Thomas Kyne was arrested for begging and Patt Conneely for breaking the window of a businessman, Mr Carr, in Eyre Square. The inquest found that they both died from 'destitution and want'.[21]

The following poem was composed by W. M. M'Comb for *Hoggs Weekly Instructor* and also published in *The Galway Vindicator*:

COME TO THE RESCUE

Remember the poor, and heed their cry,
Haste, haste to the rescue – they perish, they die!
The father lies wasted – the mother lies dead,
The little ones starving and crying for bread!
Oh! come to the rescue with heart and with hand,
For the famine is heavy and sore on the land.

Oh! ye who earth's treasures abundant possess,
Remember the poor in their time of distress,
Keep not till tomorrow the needful supply,
Today if neglected, tomorrow they die,
Oh! come to the rescue with heart and with hand,
For the famine is heavy and sore on the land.

The dead in the ditches are coffinless thrown,
The living are dying – unshrouded, unknown,
The babe is deprived of the breast of its mother,
To yield a supply to a brother or sister,
Oh! come to the rescue with heart and with hand,
For the famine is heavy and sore on the land.

The heartless to speak of improvident times,
The bygones of recklessness, folly, and crimes,

Past seasons of idleness – thus to evade,
The cry of the famishing people for aid,
Oh! come to the rescue with heart and with hand,
For the famine is heavy and sore on the land.

The man who possesseth a plentiful store,
Whose basket is full, and whose cup runneth o'er,
Yet says to his destitute brother depart,
How dwelleth God's love in his pitiless heart?
He comes not to the rescue with heart and with hand,
When the famine is heavy and sore on the land.

When the judgment of Heaven in the earth is abroad,
Let the nations be humble and hearken to God,
He smites, that the smitten may see him reveal'd,
He wounds, that the wounded may look and be heal'd,
He calls to the rescue – Oh dear withstand,
When the famine is heavy and sore on the land.[22]

10

UNRELENTING SUFFERING

The suffering continued throughout 1849. Even at this late stage 'Death from Starvation' continued to make the headlines right across the country. The following is an account of a tragedy from Enniskillen. A man named Maguire left his home to seek work to feed his two children. He was unable to secure any employment, and his neighbours, obviously in dire want themselves, were unable to or would not support the children while he was away. They both died the same day: one child in the morning and the other in the evening.[1]

The newspapers continued to publish such accounts and laid the blame on the government and, of course, the landlord system, which was bleeding the country with evictions, destitution and forced emigration. While most reports indicated a serious disregard for the people among the landlords, it is obvious from the following correspondence that some of them, acting out of either indifference or ignorance, were still not at all in touch with the reality of the situation that was causing widespread suffering all around them. Lord Clancarthy, who had published a document in support of the May Fair planned for Ballinasloe, County Galway, could not understand why people were apprehensive about attending such an event. The following comments were published in response to Clancarthy in May 1849 under the heading 'Awful Mortality in the Ballinasloe Workhouses':

> We had occasion to remark last post upon the manifesto published by Lord Clancarthy, for the purpose of having it supposed that there were 'no reasonable apprehensions' to deter persons from attending the May Fair of Ballinasloe as usual; and probably for the purpose also that his lordship should pocket his usual amount of customs. – One would think it was but the prevalence of a slight influenza he was advertising of, to allay all 'reasonable apprehension'. But what was the mortality that same week and during the May Fair, at which there need be no aspersion? Will it be believed? Do we live in a land where human life – even pauper life, is not more regarded than the life of noxious vermin? There were that week EIGHT HUNDRED AND SIXTY DEATHS IN BALLINASLOE!! – all in ONE WEEK!! This mortality, we make no doubt, after the material of starving paupers had been crowded for it to suffocation in fourteen auxiliary workhouses, will now be called a 'Visitation of Providence', as the Government are in the habit of blasphemously calling the wholesale starvation of the Irish people – ascribing to God, with demoniacal hardihood, the inhuman wickedness of their own hands.[2]

In October 1849, *The Galway Vindicator* reported that 'the English government deliberately permitted the population of Ireland to be annihilated – cleared off the surface of the country, by the unchecked progress of repeated famines, the police-supported atrocities of extermination, the appliances

Series (1): Landing troops from a gunboat in Roundstone Bay. All the images in this chapter are from a series of eviction illustrations. (*The Illustrated London News*, 1886)

of special commissions, and the willing aid of packed and partisan juries.'[3] This report may seem a little extreme, but if one considers the results of the following independent analysis of the corn being sold at one of the Galway markets, then it is easy to understand these allegations. Earlier that year, in April, samples of the government-supplied corn and meal were sent to be tested by 'eminent' people involved in the business in London. There had been numerous complaints about the corn and so it was decided to seek the advice of experts on the quality of the product being sold to the people of Ireland. There were many abuses of the system, and this was an attempt to highlight the appalling attitude and total disregard shown to the people. But, similar to other reports, it gained little credence, with the exception of the people who required help the most.

The reported findings were published in the newspapers under the heading 'The Process of Slow Poisoning: Diet of the "Mere Irish" Pauper':

My dear Sir – I have been here for nearly two hours and exhibited to several of the most eminent millers, meal-factors, and corn-factors of this country, the sample of stuff which you forwarded to me on last Monday, taken from the Relief Depot of Ballybeane, by the Rev. Mr Curley, on that day, April 23. All agree that they never saw such an article before in the London market, and that it is no wonder those who eat it should die from the use of it. I shall give you five separate reports all coming from judges of the first class.

No. 1 – It appears to be the rubble or offal of barley. Would not give it to pigs! It is quite unfit for human food.

No. 2 – It is apparently made from the husks – little or no nutriment in it. Might keep pigs alive, but no pauper in London would touch it.

No. 3 – It is the opinion of —— that the sample of meal presented by Mr MacDonnell is unfit for human food, or even for pigs. It appears to be ground barley, from which the meal has been removed. He thinks it can be no fair sample of food given to man.

No. 4 – The stuff is the refuse of mow-burned or heated barley, or barley meal. It is not fit for human food – the meal has been taken away; it is meal husk or offal.

No. 5 – Mr —— said, I think the meal must be made from the sweepings of oats and barley granaries, and is certainly unfit for human food in any civilised country.

I shall only add – which I do with perfect truth and great

Series (2): Driving on cars to the estate where the tenants are
to be evicted. (*The Illustrated London News*, 1886)

satisfaction – that among those gentlemen, certainly not fewer
than thirty or forty, who assisted or were present at the examina-
tion, there was only one pervading sentiment and expression of
sympathy for my unhappy countrymen, for whom such food was
provided, and for their condition generally.

Yours, my dear Sir, very faithfully, Eneas MacDonnell.[4]

This was not an isolated incident. In fact, a year earlier this problem had been highlighted to the local authorities in Galway. In
Connemara, it was stated that bread was not made of flour or
meal but, as the 'nursery rhyme has it, of sticks and stones and
dead men's bones'.[5] The Indian meal stores in Galway were so
deplorable that it was stated by witnesses that nothing worse than
this 'abominable stuff' could even be imagined. They said that the
'lowest description of vermin are literally abounding in it; the rats
and mice instinctively shun it, and yet this is food good enough
for human beings!' While conditions at the Orphans' Breakfast
Institute were at times deplorable, Brother Paul O'Connor found

himself in the most difficult position of having to send back to the suppliers the 'black bread' intended for the children as they would have been poisoned. There was much concern about this situation as similar incidents were being reported from many areas. There was also a lot of frustration among the benevolent societies as the very commodity that was supposed to sustain life had been turned into the instrument of its destruction. On one occasion, Brother O'Connor, upon withholding the issue of bread, remarked that it was not 'fit for human beings but for the lowest class of the animal creation'.[6] In another letter to the authorities he referred to a sample of the bread that he had sent to them for inspection and stated without exaggeration that:

> such deleterious matter is not food fit for human beings, or should I even say it is not fit for dogs … I would respectfully state, as my decided conviction, that it would be much better to put a stop to the supply, at once, and let starvation take its natural course, if not averted by Christian charity, than to peril the lives of our fellow-creatures, by setting before them as food, a species of putrid matter, upon which I have seen, with my own eyes, the black beetle and the worm luxuriating, and from which, I believe, the vilest of animals would turn away with instinctive horror.[7]

Fr Roche also wrote to the authorities regarding the food being supplied to the boys attending the 'Male Free School'. He stated that the bread supplied by the British Association, another organisation supplying support for the famine, was 'rank poison' and that if any of the children had eaten it there would have been a case of 'homicide' to answer.[8] The British Associa-

Series (3): Surgeon of the force examining the sick wife of a tenant.
(*The Illustrated London News*, 1886)

tion came in for criticism on a number of occasions, as did the
Union inspector, Major M'Kie, and while they were at times
careless, they were for the most part doing their best. Major
M'Kie in fact died from fever contracted in the workhouse; he
was buried in the grounds of St Nicholas' Collegiate church on
18 June 1849.[9] Both of the following accounts were reported to
the town commissioners, the first in March and the second in
July 1849:

(1)   The Government Commissariat Stores are groaning under
a load of damaged rye-meal and other bread-stuffs, fit only for
sale by auction for the feeding of swine; yet their honours, the
Commissioners of Poor Laws, deem it sufficiently good for the
starving population of the 'Citie of the Tribes'. To the credit of

the Vice-Guardians be it said, they have charitably remonstrated against the use of such deleterious stuff; yet, upon the report of Major M'Kie, Inspecting Officer of the Union, it is to be called out to active service, and used for out-door relief.

Well, the people are all but starved, next fed with 'food for dogs', then taxed and robbed to boot. Mark! This rye-meal to be used, taken from the Commissary Stores, will, through the Commissary, be charged to the Union at the price of an honest merchantable article. It is to be baked into bread at an expense of 35s. or 40s. per ton, a further humbug, to hide the gross deception. The over-burdened tax-payers of the Union must pay all. Why not give meal or flour as out-door relief; the recipients are not without means of cooking the crude article. No, this would not answer their purpose. The imposition would be too soon detected. On Wednesday next we shall see if this horrible transaction will be persevered in. As Major M'Kie and the Vice-Guardians are not very harmonious upon the subject, we hope the public will benefit by a split in the camp.[10]

(2) This week another specimen of this abominable stuff has been left at our office, in the hope that we may call for enquiry into the facts with a view to ascertaining whether the lives of starving multitudes or the profits of contractors ought to be taken most into account. We do most positively assert that in some department or other – let us not be supposed at involving the Vice-Guardian of the Union, they have nothing to do with the matter – but, other officials must have grossly neglected their duties of overseeing the quality of bread supplied from the stuff of the Commissariat store. It is a mixture of ingredients most offensive

Series (4): Troops jumping over a stream on the march.
(*The Illustrated London News*, 1886)

to the smell, most nauseous to the taste, and, as we are assured, most pernicious in its effect on human life. Nay, so bad has it proved to be that, a gentleman having purchased a quantity as food for swine, it was refused by them and was in the end thrown into the sea. The British Association should look to the matter, or the people may have reason to exclaim of them.[11]

Towards the end of 1849, the people in the forefront of the fight against hunger and disease were extremely weary; Fr Roche fought tirelessly for social justice through the famine years and never refused to attend the enormous number of 'sick calls' placed on him. He was, by this time, exhausted and worn down physically and mentally, but despite being so weakened and disillusioned he never gave up his fight. He survived the famine but died on 18 April 1867 having contracted typhus.[12]

Throughout the famine years, these people were delighted with any support and encouraged many benevolent organisations to help in any way possible. On 21 October 1849, the Galway branch of the Saint Vincent de Paul Society was founded at Lombard Street. They had been invited to set up a branch in October 1847, but because of their already huge workload they were unable to do so at the time. Their first meeting took place close to Brother Paul O'Connor's Breakfast Institute.[13] The situation proved a serious test for the Saint Vincent de Paul Society, but they rose to the challenge and set about their caring work immediately, and, although it was overwhelming, they continued in the forefront of the fight against hunger as the year closed.

Another Christmas came and went without much joy for the poor. Even going into the New Year of 1850 gave little hope. There had been so many disappointments; what would make this year any different? Hunger and destitution were never far away during bitter cold winters, and this year was no different.

Eviction was dreaded and loomed over the heads of most underprivileged people continually; what was even more shocking was when clergymen became involved in this terrible business. In January 1850, Revd John Treanor, accompanied by the sub-sheriff, proceeded to dispossess some forty families of their homes in Galway. He had been appointed agent by the landlord, and the following is an account of the proceedings:

Series (5): Clearing out a tenant's furniture.
(*The Illustrated London News*, 1886)

We were not spectators of the sad scene, but the account given of it by one who had been an eye witness of the whole transaction, was truly dismal. It ought to be sufficient to move the most remorseless heart to pity, to see hearths quenched, and, with them, the few surviving hopes of the miserable beings once cheerful assembled around them. In the chill month of January, how mournful is it to behold in a Christian land, women and children, houseless and homeless, thrown upon the world, with scarcely a sufficiency of rags upon their famished and famine-wasted bodies to cover their nakedness! Can any fireside affection dwell in the breasts of men, capable of perpetrating an act of such enormity, during such a season, and at a period of such crying distress. We quarrel not with the landlord who, by every fair and equitable means, endeavours to collect his rents; nor is it our desire to animadvert with the severity of the conduct of Mr Treanor on the present occasion.

Series (6): The sheriff giving possession to the bailiff, handing him a wisp of straw from the thatched roof. (*The Illustrated London News*, 1886)

But, for the sake of religion, and the respect due to its ministers, we could wish that clergymen of all denominations would stand aloof from any participation in acts of oppression against the persecuted poor, of whose rights and privileges, it is their duty to stand boldly forth as the guardians and defenders. Surely, all our readers would agree with us when we say that a Vicar of St Nicholas – a dean of Queen's College – and a Land Agent, 'tria juncta in uno' form an odd compound. The duty of the former two offices, properly discharged, would give ample employment for the rev. gentleman's time, without his undertaking the additional and arduous labours of a Land Steward, his debut, in which character has not been calculated to increase his popularity in Galway.[14]

The condemnation and the disturbing accounts continued to be ignored by members of government, which gave rise to the following comments in July 1850 when *The Galway Vindicator* stated that the Irish peasants had been 'degraded and despised in this the land of their fathers … They have been allowed to languish and die of hunger in the midst of plenty.'[15]

Throughout 1850 there was no end to the number of paupers coming into the town, and the misery of these poor 'unfriended outcasts' was harrowing, even at this late stage of the famine. The people of the town had also suffered dreadfully but had grown accustomed to the regular influx of homeless people. In December it was reported that two miserable-looking 'half-naked' children were found huddled together sitting on a

Series (7): An evicted peasant family.
(*The Illustrated London News*, 1886)

footpath. All they had to protect themselves from the cold and wet ground was a 'handful of straw' on which they had spent the previous night. The winter conditions prevailed, causing them 'unrelenting suffering'.[16]

The town commissioners were under extreme pressure from the situation facing them on a daily basis. They had to contend with the additional problems of 'filth' accumulating on the streets of the town. There was also an accumulation of 'manure in the lanes and alleys' which was adding to the already serious health problems. The main streets were not much better, with mud and filth being allowed to build up for the want of cleaning. They were worried that businesspeople visiting the town would not be encouraged to invest when they witnessed the conditions that prevailed in Galway. The street hygiene problems were exacerbated by the number of vagrants roaming the streets; it was proving impossible to cope with.[17]

Although conditions were appalling in the town, most of the vagrants, even during this late period, were avoiding the workhouse, which would indicate that circumstances in this establishment were worse than ever. Having said this, the workhouse was still having problems because of overcrowding. The staff members were finding it difficult to cope, and some of the younger 'pauper' women were now acting as nurses. There were obviously problems among the staff, as the matron was once caught in a drunken state. In addition, she was accused of being too 'familiar' with the paupers. Because of this, the authorities wanted to have her dismissed. However, owing to her excellent work and dedication to duty, other members of staff defended her, and she managed to hold on to her position.[18] In fact, the

Series (8): Marching to another eviction.
(*The Illustrated London News*, 1886)

matron had no choice but to be 'familiar' with the paupers as she now had some of them working for her.

The weekly deaths recorded in the Galway Union that year were still averaging twenty-five people.[19] Given the horrors endured by the people, it is surprising that there was so little violence. However, there were some landlords shot, and there was general unrest in some areas, which is documented in the next chapter.

The following poem, which finishes with a pledge to uphold an English cause if support was forthcoming for Ireland, was published in *The Galway Mercury* in 1847:

THE APPEAL OF THE IRISH POOR

Assail'd by hunger, cold, and death,
O whither shall we fly?
Throughout the world, the length and breadth,
Is heard our doleful cry!

O where doth Pity dwell? for there,
We'd made our woes still known;
At home? – abroad? – or high on fair,
Britannia's noble Throne?

Yet Pity dwells at home, abroad,
And on Britannia's Throne,
We gratefully confess, and laud,
Past kindness to us shown.

But ne'er the poor of Erin felt,
Such want as now we feel,
Our sorrows are enough to melt,
The hardest hearts of steel.

The hand of God is on us laid,
For bread our children cry,
O pity take? and quickly aid,
Or else we starve – we die!

Oh say not we exaggerate,
But quickly come to save,
We justly fear our brethren's fate,
Who've an early grave.

They'er gone! and daily still they go,
To save them not a friend!
Let Britain and the world know,
STARVATION was their end!

And still Starvation stalks abroad,
Then hearken, while we call,
Ye friends of man – ye friends of God,
We now appeal to ALL.

Ye Mothers! We to you appeal,
Whose tender bosoms swell,
With pity, for our children feel,
None else can feel so well!

Ye Ministers of every name!
If blest with competence,
Give, while you charity proclaim,
And use your influence.

Ye Wealthy! come with lib'ral hand,
And share the golden store,
Ye Irish Great Ones, save your land,
And help the starving poor!

And thou, O Britain! for us feel,
Think o'er our fathers dead,
Who fac'd the cannon and the steel,
And for thy glory bled.

Their sons and daughters on thee call,
Whose fathers sav'd thy throne,
Whose brethren in thy ranks still fall,
Their valour thou must own.

O Britain! think of Erin then,

Relieve her misery,

And Erin's sons will bleed again,

And nobly die for thee![20]

Series (9): Straw hut on the mountainside, the only shelter after eviction.
(*The Illustrated London News*, 1886)

11

BACKLASH AND REBELLION

It was inevitable that violence would erupt at some stage given such suffering. The 'Whiteboys' had been active for many years, and there were a number of incidents of violence during the famine involving them. 'Whiteboy' was a term first used to describe political agitators in October 1761. They were small disorganised groups of rebels who sought to redress various grievances against landlords and the authorities. From the 1760s to the 1840s they were responsible for attacks all across rural Ireland. They derived their name from the white smocks their members wore during night-time raids. There were other underground movements throughout this period with similar objectives, but almost all of them are now referred to as Whiteboys. Their objectives were to have rents, tithes and clergy dues reduced and to have wages increased for labourers and small tenant farmers. They wanted to put an end to 'land grabbing' by large landowners, as it was forcing the poor from the land. They normally issued a 'proclamation' or 'law' which was, in effect, a warning to anyone who they believed was guilty of these 'offences' that action would be taken against them if they continued to exploit the poor. If these warnings were ignored, then the proclamation would be enforced by violence and intimidation. This action included destruction of property, mutilation of animals, warning shots fired through windows and physical assaults.

After the 1790s, the movements became progressively more violent, and a number of people lost their lives in attacks by Whiteboys.[1] One of the most renowned of these attacks occurred in 1820 when Anthony Daly was accused of the attempted assassination of James Hardiman Burke, the landlord at St Clerans near Craughwell, County Galway. Burke was Mayor of Galway at the time so this was also viewed as a direct assault on his authority. After his conviction, Daly was executed on the hill of Seefin, a few miles from Craughwell.[2] The incident is still very much alive in that area, and a monument in memory of Daly was erected on the site of the execution during the 1950s. Despite this type of deterrent, Whiteboy activity continued and became even more daring.

The onslaught of the Great Famine signalled the end of the Whiteboy movement as it devastated the social class that populated its ranks. They did manage to perpetrate some minor attacks during the famine, such as an incident at Ballingarry in 1847, when they clashed with a group of police. Both sides were armed, resulting in one policeman being wounded, a Whiteboy being shot dead and two others arrested. Later that year, a policeman was killed at Croom and another wounded in an ambush.[3] Some landlords became so concerned about their safety that they had policemen stationed in their homes. David Wilson of Belvoir House in County Clare was one such land-lord. He obviously suspected that he was in danger, and a short time after the police took up duty at his home the Whiteboys made their move. Upon forcing their way into the house they were shocked to find themselves confronted by armed police, and four of them were captured.[4]

By the end of the famine there was only a shadow of the movement still in existence, and this was limited to remote rural areas. Many of the Whiteboys had emigrated, and, in a sense, they continued the struggle in the USA where they became known as the Molly Maguires and were involved in resistance against exploitative powerful industrialists.

When one considers the situation in Ireland, it is amazing that there was not a lot more violence. Hungry people can be a difficult force to deal with, as the French aristocracy found to their cost in Paris in 1789 when the French Revolution was sparked off. While most sources indicate that there was little famine on mainland Europe after 1846, and this is true for the most part, there were, nonetheless, food riots abroad right up to at least 1847. Food shortages were reported from most parts of Germany, Belgium, Denmark and Sweden, causing much unrest. In Stuttgart, people took to the streets, damaging government property; they set up barricades and demanded 'Liberty and Bread'. The King himself became involved in trying to restore order, and, accompanied by Frederick, the Prince Royal, he visited the main streets where some 2,000 soldiers had taken up positions. The people were in no mood for talk; they demanded food and began to shower the soldiers with stones. The troops retaliated and a number of people were killed by gunfire and the barricades were taken by force. In other areas of the city, stores, shops and businesses were attacked in search of food. It

Bread riots in Germany, 1847. (*The Illustrated London News*, 1847)

was reported that thousands of women had joined together and plundered carts of flour and corn, which were being taken to the various markets. Several detachments of infantry and four batteries of artillery were called in to bring the situation under control.[5]

England also experienced food riots. Devonshire, Cornwall and Somerset were all affected in 1847 by people taking to the streets. Large crowds, mainly women, went on the rampage in Exeter. Bakeries, butcher shops, corn stores and markets were all attacked. It is interesting to note that the women were not trying to steal the food but were demanding that it be sold at the correct price. As in Ireland, merchants were cashing in on the plight of the people and had almost doubled the price of all foodstuffs. The Yeomanry Cavalry was called in to take charge of the situation. Similar riots also broke out across the west of England that same year. However, even the hardship experienced in these countries fades significantly when it is compared with the Irish story.[6]

The landlords in Ireland had good reason to fear for their safety as anti-landlord feeling grew even more bitter during the famine years. This bitterness resulted in the shooting dead of six landlords and ten others involved in land management during this period. Among them was Major Denis Mahon of County Roscommon. He was a cavalry officer in the British army who had inherited property in Strokestown shortly before the famine. Mahon's death came against a backdrop of land clearances, evictions and forced emigration on coffin ships. When news of his killing was circulated around the county, bonfires burnt for miles in celebration of his death. Fr Michael McDermott, the parish priest of Strokestown, was accused of inciting the act of terror against Mahon. The priest did criticise the manner in which Mahon had treated his tenants. He almost defended the shooting, saying that it had been caused by his own 'infamous and inhuman cruelties' carried out against a tenantry already 'wound up to woeful and vengeful exasperation by the loss of their exiled relatives, as well as by hunger and pestilence'.[7] McDermott's Bishop, Dr George Brown, investigated the allegations against him and dismissed them. He also published a list of 3,006 dispossessed tenants whom Mahon and his agents had evicted, and added the comment, 'most of whom are now dead'.[8]

After the assassination of Mahon, British officials became

very concerned and were extremely fearful that the violence might spread. This resulted in an additional 15,000 troops being sent to Ireland. They also passed the Crime and Outrage Bill, curtailing certain liberties in Ireland, such as the carrying of firearms. Despite these safety measures, many Anglo-Irish landowners and gentry fled the country in fear for their lives. Those who did remain utilised heavy police protection.[9]

The Young Irelanders organised a rebellion for 1848 without the knowledge of the vast majority of Irish people.[10] The Young Ireland movement, under the leadership of William Smith O'Brien and Thomas Francis Meagher, was inspired by nationalism on mainland Europe. They had visited Paris to congratulate the French leaders on their new Republic. Meagher returned to Ireland with the tricolour flag; it was to be a symbol of reconciliation between the Orange and Green, and a united front against the government. O'Brien believed he could accomplish similar results in Ireland as had been achieved in France. They hoped to unite Irish landlords and tenants in protest against British rule and began planning an uprising for the autumn of 1848. However, the government speeded up the revolt on 22 July 1848 by announcing the suspension of habeas corpus, which meant that members of the Young Ireland movement could be arrested and imprisoned without trial. O'Brien decided that rather than let the government arrest the leaders he would have to make an immediate stand. On 23 July O'Brien and Meagher travelled throughout Wexford, Kilkenny and Tipperary in an effort to encourage rebellion. On 28 July they had barricades erected outside the village of The Commons, County Tipperary, to prevent the police from arresting them. As the situation developed, O'Brien and Meagher were joined by a group of local Young Ireland supporters.

When the police arrived, they decided not to engage the rebels and turned down another road, avoiding the barricades. Upon seeing the police reaction, the rebels followed them, crossing some fields. There were forty-six police under the command of Sub-Inspector Trant. The police barricaded themselves into a large two-storey farmhouse, taking five young children in the house as hostages, and prepared to defend their position. The house was the property of Margaret McCormack, a widow, who was not at home when the police arrived. Upon her return, she requested access to her home and asked the police to leave; they refused and would not release the children either. The house was then surrounded by the rebels, creating a stand-off.

Before any violence broke out, O'Brien and Margaret McCormack made their way to the parlour window of the house to speak with the police. While trying to negotiate terms, O'Brien said to Sub-Inspector Trant, 'We are all Irishmen – give up your guns and you are free to go.' O'Brien even shook hands with some of the policemen through the window. It seems that progress was being made until a constable fired a shot at O'Brien while he was in negotiations. This immediately sparked off an exchange of fire between the police and the rebels. O'Brien was dragged out of the line of fire by two of his men, James Stephens and Terence Bellew MacManus, both of whom were wounded in the exchange. The rebels at the front of the house, along with some women and children who had gathered around, curious as to what was going on, crouched for cover behind the wall. One man, Thomas Walsh, tried to cross between the gate posts but was shot dead by the police. Another man, Patrick McBride, who had been standing at the gable end of the house when the firing began, was fatally wounded by the police as he tried to follow his retreating companions. The gun battle went on for a number of hours, and during lulls in the firing the rebels retreated out of the range of police fire.

Later that day, another party of police arrived from Cashel; the rebels attempted to engage them but had to abort this action as they were low on ammunition. The police realised this and continued to advance, firing as they moved forward. It quickly became evident that the police in the house would soon be reinforced and rescued. This situation forced the rebels into a full retreat which effectively terminated both the era of the Young Irelanders and the idea of repeal.[11] The short and totally ineffective rebellion later became known as the 'Battle of the Widow McCormack's Cabbage Garden'.

The siege of Widow McCormack's house.
(*The Illustrated London News*, 1848)

While the rebellion was a failure, it did highlight to the authorities the threat to security. William Smith O'Brien was born at Dromoland, County Clare, in 1803, the year of Robert Emmet's rebellion.[12] He was always outspoken on the political situation in Ireland and constantly made his views known. He was arrested on 6 August 1848 for his part in the rebellion and tried at a special sitting of the district court at Clonmel, County Tipperary. He was found guilty and sentenced to death. However, the sentence caused serious concerns among all segments of the Irish community, which eventually resulted in his death sentence being commuted to transportation for life.[13]

Thomas Francis Meagher was born in Waterford in 1823. He was also tried for treason and was sentenced to transportation to Tasmania, along with two other rebels and O'Brien. Later there was great concern among the Irish over the harsh treatment of O'Brien while on board the transportation ship.

Tasmania was a brutal colony, and in the early months of 1852 Meagher escaped to America. He landed in San Francisco and later made his way to New York.[14] He eventually became a brigadier general with the Irish Brigade of the Union army and gained a powerful reputation as a soldier during the American Civil War. O'Brien made an unsuccessful attempt to escape from Maria Island off Tasmania. In 1854, he was released on the condition that he would never return to Ireland. He sailed to Europe and settled in Brussels. In 1856, he was granted an unconditional pardon, and, following this, he returned to Ireland, but played no further part in politics. His contribution to Ireland was not forgotten in Galway city where a bridge was named after him. The building of this structure also gave employment when it was most needed. O'Brien's Bridge was completed in 1851 and replaced the older Great West Bridge, which had served Galway for centuries. It had been repaired many times but by the 1840s a more solid structure was required. As with many other projects and issues of the day, Fr Peter Daly was involved; he actually laid the foundation stone for the new bridge. During his speech, he delivered an address on the future prospects of the town, proposed a toast to its prosperity and hoped for a better future for Ireland and its people. He then gave the workmen fifteen sovereigns between them to celebrate.[15]

Just over a month before the 1848 rebellion, the following poem by J.T. appeared in *The Galway Vindicator*:

COURAGE BROTHERS

Courage Brothers, right before us,
Lies the path to sure success,
Freedoms day is breaking o'er us,
Soon her light her toils shall bless,
Though a gallant few may suffer,
Death or exile in her cause,
Thousands still remain to love her,
Disregarding foreign laws.

Often to uphold a stranger,
Irish blood has run like rain,
Irish hearts have death and danger,
Braved on many foreign plain,

And if this were oft repeated,
For the fading wreath of fame,
And we now had hesitated,
Shame were ours – eternal shame!

Oh my brothers, look around you,
Tell me what you witness, save,
Scenes that daily, hourly wound you,
Thousands sinking to the grave,
All unpitied, nay derided –
This dear country of our birth,
Which we love, in which we prided,
Made a land of plague and death!

Onward, then, look around you,
Mark me, now we wage a strife,
Not for country, home, or altar,
But for food – aye food of life,
If we fall – we scape starvation,
If we conquer – our's the boast,
To have raised this Irish nation,
When despised degraded most.[16]

12

ESCAPE FROM FAMINE

The scale of the disaster was so enormous that it devastated communities and villages across the country, forcing thousands of peasants to make their way to the big towns, particularly to port towns such as Galway. Thousands died making the gruelling walk to the ports, many of them without even being accorded the most basic acknowledgement of a marked grave. Many towns and villages shunned these people out of fear of disease, terrified of the sights they witnessed entering their community daily. The only salvation for many was the dangerous and sometimes appalling voyage that had to be endured by those trying to escape starvation, disease and death. The ships that serviced Ireland during those years were widely branded 'coffin ships' because of the appalling death toll and disease associated with them. Many were mere freight vessels that had been converted to carry passengers. Some were vessels which merchants no longer entrusted to carry 'valuable' cargos. Accommodation on these ships consisted of hastily built and improvised bunks which utilised every inch of space. Of course this meant that some ships were overloaded beyond the limits of safety, and this also resulted in the lower compartments being places of terrible misery. Some shipowners took advantage of the situation and increased their profits by providing as little food as possible, working just inside the legal requirements. Because of this, many people had to rely on the charity of fellow passengers if they had no supplies themselves. Some owners disobeyed the law entirely and allowed the vessels to be overcrowded for sheer profit. Many of the passengers were already weakened by hunger and suffered from malnutrition and other famine-related illnesses. This resulted in the spread of disease on board, adding to the terrible hardships people had already endured.

It has been estimated that about one-fifth of those who sailed from Irish shores during the famine perished en route. Those who died during the voyage were consigned to the bottom of the sea. Sometimes these ships were also short-handed in manpower, and during gales male passengers were forced to carry out the work of sailors. The voyage to America normally took about six to eight weeks in favourable conditions; however, during bad weather the journey could take up to twelve weeks.[1]

Conditions were so horrendous on board some ships that a Canadian official once remarked to a priest there that it would be more humane to send a battery from Quebec to sink the ships rather than to allow the passengers to suffer in such an agonising manner. The healthy were also getting sick because of being forced to live among the dying and the dead. A priest, Fr Taschereau, commented on the foul air he was forced to breathe between the decks of a ship he was visiting. He said that the flooring was covered with muck, and when speaking of the rations he stated that it was unwholesome food and dirty water.

Taschereau observed a child playing with the hand of its dead mother. Another priest, Fr Hubert Robson, said that he would give his life for 'those unfortunates'; this statement came after he went down into the hold of a ship where he was walking ankle-deep in slime.

d Connaught Advertiser

AMERICA

FOR THE FLOURISHING CITY OF
BOSTON.
THE FINE AMERICAN SHIP
"THALIA",

500 Tons Burthen, Capt. PATTEN, Commander,
Will sail for the above port on the 21th day of May
next, weather permitting.

THIS Splendid Vessel will be amply supplied with Provisions, Fuel and Water, and every attention will paid to the comfort of the passengers by the captain and crew during the voyage.

For passage fare application to be made to
J. B. PURDON, Victoria place.
J. DUFFY, Ballyglass, or
EDMOND DUFFY,
Back-street and New Dock, Galway.

Galway, May 5, 1849.

Thalia of Boston, ship advertisement.
(*The Galway Vindicator*, 1849)

Many people making their way to America and Canada travelled to Liverpool on the first leg of the journey. In 1847, the *Naomi*, carrying Irish emigrants from Liverpool, docked in Grosse Isle. Seventy-eight of the 331 passengers had died on the voyage, and 104 were sick.[2] The *Loosthank*, also out of Liverpool, lost 117 passengers of its 348. Thirty-five more people died within three days of arriving in Canada, and most of the crew were also sick. Overall, only twenty people escaped the sickness on this ship. The *Lady Constable* lost twenty-three people en route. The *Montreal Pilot*, reporting on the 'doomed people of Ireland', stated that thousands of them had found graves on the banks of the St Lawrence:

> far far from the friends of their childhood … Alas! no mother's hand closed the pallid lip of the dying; – neither brothers nor sisters heard the last agonising struggle of the spirit, eager to free herself from her loathsome prison, and wing her flight to the kingdom of her Creator.[3]

Additional problems arose when ships were refused permission to land passengers in the USA. This caused extreme anxiety among the unfortunate emigrants. In 1847, the brig *Serph* was turned away from Boston with all its passengers, among them 118 cases of fever. They were ordered to go to New Brunswick or any other British port in Canada. When the passengers tried to leave the ship they were forcibly driven back. Similarly, the brig *Mary* from Cork was turned away and told to go to Halifax in Nova Scotia, causing the passengers to riot; the trouble was brought under control by force of arms.[4] In the same year, the Anglican Bishop of Montreal, George Mountain, visited Grosse Isle to see the plight of the emigrants being landed there. He was shocked by what he witnessed as he felt that the reports must have been exaggerated. In one of the tents he found a dying child covered with vermin. The body of another little boy was found under a tree where he had sat down to rest. Hundreds of children were orphaned, and it became the task of the Catholic charities of Montreal and Quebec to look after them until they could find adoptive homes in Canada.[5]

Over 100 ships serviced Galway between the years 1845 and 1850. The weekly newspapers carried ships' advertisements and encouraged people to emigrate. By May 1847, the authorities were unable to say just how many passengers had left the port of Galway in the previous two months, but they did state that it far exceeded the full sailing season of any previous year.[6] Free passage to New South Wales with provisions and medical care provided during the voyage was offered to agricultural labourers, shepherds, farm servants and female domestic staff of 'good character'. There was also the promise of increased wages upon landing. Emigration to New South Wales had been suspended in 1844, but by 1847 it had become 'urgent' to supply additional workers to the colony.[7] The poem 'An Emigrant's Farewell' included at the end of this chapter, captures the thoughts of some of these emigrants.

Among the ships that serviced Galway on a regular basis was the *Cushlamachree*. This ship was owned by Patrick Lynch of Galway. It is not clear if any passengers were lost off this ship, but it did experience some rough and harrowing crossings. On

2 January 1849, it sailed out of Galway, bound for New York, carrying 119 passengers. It ran into terrible weather conditions from the very beginning, and the passengers had to endure a brutal eight-week voyage, most of which was spent below deck. It eventually docked in New York on 1 March 1849 and offloaded its frightened and sickly human cargo.[8]

Crew members on some ships were absolutely brutal towards the Irish emigrants. On the emigrant ship *Washington*, which sailed from Liverpool on 27 October 1850, 'A delicate old man named John M'Corcoran', who was stooping down while trying to wash his socks, was given a 'severe kick' into the back by the First Mate. Such was the force of the attack that the poor man was left lying on the deck and passed blood over the following days. This was not an isolated incident; there were many unprovoked attacks by other crew members. One passenger wrote a letter of complaint to the Captain regarding this attack, who then asked him to read it aloud. Before he finished reading the letter, the Captain became very abusive and began calling the man names, telling him that he would put him in irons for the remainder of the voyage. The First Mate then punched the man and threw him onto the deck. The following is an extract from the letter, which was signed by 120 passengers; many others were terrified to sign as they feared for their safety:

SHIP *WASHINGTON*, OFF NEW YORK, DEC. 2, 1850.
We testify, as a warning to, and for the sake of, future emigrants, that the passengers on board this noble ship *Washington*, Commander A. Page, have been treated in a brutal manner by its officers, and that we have not received one-half the quantity provisions allowed

by act of parliament, and stipulated for us in our contract tickets … Four entire days having expired since the day on which the ship was appointed to sail, and three entire days since it actually sailed from the port of Liverpool, without our having water, and many of us having no provisions to meet such an emergency, we request that you will inform us when we may expect to commence receiving the allowance which is our due.

Vere Foster.[9]

While there were many horror stories told of the sea voyages throughout the famine period, not many of them could equal the absolute brutality and callousness revealed in the following account. It raises the question of 'man's inhumanity to man' and leaves one under no illusion as to how certain individuals in positions of power scorned the Irish paupers and even hastened their deaths. Under the heading 'Most Cruel Inhumanity at Sea: Is It Murder?', this letter was first sent to the editor of the *Freeman* and afterwards published in *The Galway Vindicator*:

Sir – With a view to the public good I forward you an extract from the letter of a passenger on board the —— Captain —— from Liverpool to New York, in the months of July and August last. *Juverna*. – I left Liverpool on Friday, the 13th of July. We were four or five days out before we lost sight of Ireland. In about four days more of the cholera broke out carrying away every one that caught it – in the first three days fifteen were swept away. – There was nothing but consternation on board; the captain wrote out a notice, and posted it up, to observe cleanliness, but it was all to no purpose, the cholera continued to rage for a week or more. It went away then, but not till it cut off nineteen or twenty. The people got into good spirits, but it did not last long, the cholera reappeared amongst us, the people began to die very fast, and as soon as the breath appeared to leave the body they were that instant thrown over (I use the word *appeared*, for I think some of them were alive, their limbs being as pliant as ever). We lost in all, I think, 38 or 32 – eight of them were sailors. We lost our mate and carpenter, and had two sailors sick during the whole voyage, and the passengers had to work as sailors. I myself was on watch on deck three whole nights.

We lost one of our passengers over board – he and some others were sitting in the life-boat, in the middle of the vessel where you would imagine there was no danger. The boat was on a kind of deck raised on a level with the quarter deck. One of the sails was flapping backward and forward, and a rope attached to it swinging about, which caught him under the arm, and the sail giving a sudden flap, it launched him right into the sea; his foot touched the side of the vessel as he went head foremost. I happened to be sitting on the quarter deck, and saw all that went forward. When I saw him fall I ran to the back of the wheel-house, where I knew buoys were kept, and cast one towards him; but the vessel had passed on, and the buoy was seen floating within a perch of him, and he swimming very well to gain it.

We were going at a rate of ten or twelve miles an hour; the captain was called up from his cabin, and he gave some orders to have the sails taken down. After a little pulling he desired the sailors to set the sails right again, and on we went, leaving poor Joseph Kavanagh to paddle about in the waves. One man said he watched him for about half a mile, and could plainly see him above the water. I think he must have reached the buoy; if so, what must have been his reflections on seeing the departure of the vessel, and left to see or hear nothing but the ocean waves rolling about him?[10]

AN EMIGRANT'S FAREWELL

You ask me to sing when my bosom is breaking,
You bid me cheer up when my spirit is low,
But who can be gay when his heart strings are aching,
And his soul is crushed down by a mountain of woe?

Then, blame me not friends, if the heart's core within me,
Is crushed at the parting of you friend, and you,
If pleasure from pain hath no power to win me,
When thus on the eve of a final adieu.

As musings spring up me soul's recollections,
Like evening's mild beam on the breast of the brae,
A sinking comes o'er me – a death like dejection,
That turns me in darkness from joy thoughts far away.

And here, with my friends for the last time about me,
The comrades of youth, honest, truthful, and tried,
Who failed not, who quailed not, when others did flout me,
Oh! – must I not mourn to be torn from their side?

And when I look round on the loved land that bore me,
The blue of her mountains – the green of her meads,
The waters and wood wildly waving before me,
Ev'ry vein in my bosom painfully bleeds.

It wrings me to go from the stormy Benedar,
From Tara of Kings – from the friendly Fingall,
But leaving them still 'neath the hungry invader,
Is darker, and darker, and sadder than all.

But, here I bequeath them my blessing for ever,
And gladly would leave them my blood and my bones,
But vain is the offering – no human endeavour,
Can make them start up from their gloom and their groans.

Then here, take my hand, for this night we'll be parted,
To meet no more o'er the flow of the Pell,
And soul-seared and sadly, and bruised, broken hearted,
I bid you farewell friends – for ever farewell.[11]

13

VOYAGE OF HOPE
AND DISASTER

By 1849, emigrants were being encouraged to purchase a book, *The Life of Franklin*. It came highly recommended and cost 1 shilling. It promised to give the emigrant a better knowledge of the New World, where 'knowledge is absolute power', where a man, 'however humble', can reach any rank of society. It gave examples of emigrants who had been successful in America. It was available for sale in port towns and could be read during the voyage, where the reader was advised to lose no time and to exercise his 'powers of observation' among his fellow passengers.[1]

Emigrants were also advised not to take unnecessary commodities with them. The general rule was to take as little as possible, except for money – this was most important to have available. There were currency exchange issues for those who had money; the advice was simple, take 'sovereigns as they can be used in any part of the United States'.[2] Clothes and tools were also important to take on the voyage, but only necessary clothing and essential tools. Emigrants were advised to purchase 'loosely fitting overcoats' which would be useful for the voyage and would also protect them from the intense American winters. 'Stout boots' and shoes were a must for the traveller. Many people were unsure of the reception that they would receive upon arrival at their destination and again the advice was simple:

> Go, by all means – leave this land of misery; but, yet, prepare yourselves for all sorts of disappointments. You are Irish – you belong to the soil of the Saints – you have been bred in the land of religion and simplicity – you now begin the world, take care of the stranger. Be sober, be cool, be religious, be industrious. The best men of our country are going, and where the tide of emigration will end, we know not … America is the ground where wages may be had, and where industry, talent, and energy will have its reward.[3]

It was reported in 1849 that the emigration numbers for the previous year were almost 300,000 people; this did not include those who sailed from Liverpool or from any of the other English ports, nor did it include those forced to seek employment in England and Scotland. The authorities predicted that the emigration numbers for 1849 would far exceed those of 1848. They also noted a striking contrast between the people of previous years and the new emigrants. In the earlier years people were driven from Ireland by famine, hardship and landlords whilst many of the later emigrants were people of substance and station in their localities and were leaving voluntarily. This became worrying and disheartening for the authorities as they felt that the country was now being depleted of all classes. With such losses of youth and manpower it would take years for the country to recover even when the famine was finally over.[4]

In June 1850, it was announced that the steamer *Viceroy* was to sail from Galway to New York, opening a new era in the west of Ireland, and a welcome development for all concerned as this was the first steamer to service Galway.[5] At the time steamers were considered to be a safer method of travel than the coffin ships, which relied on the wind. Of course, reports of gold being discovered in California encouraged more healthy young emigrants to leave the country. Even reports that a lead mine of 'rare value' had been discovered near Gort, County Galway, and that its silver ore was richer than the South American mines, did not stem the flow of people out of the ports.[6]

When the emigration ships *Clarence*, *Elizabeth* and *David* sailed out of the port of Galway in April 1849, they were carrying some 400 passengers between them.[7] The following account was written by a *Galway Vindicator* reporter and clearly shows that by this time the healthiest young people were indeed fleeing the country:

Emigration – There are few so dispirited scenes to be witnessed now as the stream of emigration. It momentarily dashes away the hopes of regenerating this country. Looking upon it we must naturally enquire what is to be done when the industry, and health and strength of the land will have passed away; and the few who would still, through patriotism, cling to 'the sinking ship' can scarce but envy the resolution of those they see depart – the Israelites on their exodus from bondage and pauperism. Such must naturally have been the reflections of any thoughtful person upon departure of the *Sea Bird* from our quays on Monday evening last. The very heart of our country, so far as it could contain, seemed departing –

the youthful peasantry of both sexes, well-dressed, healthful, and, we may add, cheerful, bidding adieu for ever to the country that has been a country of suffering and misfortune. It was sorrowful to look upon them apparently, under the circumstances, so happy. To the number of about 400 they departed, accompanied by a Catholic clergyman, who had been driven as they had by the destitution and calamities around, to seek a livelihood in America.[8]

AMERICA.

FOR THE

FLOURISHING CITY OF

NEW YORK,

THE SPLENDID NEW SHIP

" SEA BIRD," OF GALWAY ;

J. M'DONAGH, MASTER,—1,000 TONS BURTHEN,

Will Sail for the above port on or about

The 7th day of August next,

Weather permitting).

THE above Ship is built of the best materials, coppered and copper-fastened, and warranted a fast sailer, and will be fitted up in a most commodious manner for the accommodation of Cabin and Steerage passengers. This truly lucky vessel landed her passengers all in good health, this season, after a most agreeable passage of 20 days.

The Sea Bird will be amply supplied with Fuel, Water and Provisions according to act of Parliament. The well-known experience and proverbial attention of Captain M'Donogh to his passengers render this vessel a most desirable one for emigrants as there are many Berths already engaged, application should be made, at once, to the Captain, on board ; or to

J. & A. IRELAND,

Eyre-square, Galway,

Who are now discharging from on board the Sea Bird 700 Tons YELLOW INDIAN CORN, which they offer for Sale on moderate terms.

Galway, July 7, 1849.

Sea Bird of Galway, ship advertisement.
(*The Galway Vindicator*, 1849)

One of the greatest dangers at sea, and the most terrifying for emigrants, was the chance of being shipwrecked. The brig *St. John* which sailed from Galway in September 1849 ran into a terrible storm and suffered disastrous loss of life when it sank off the coast of Cohasset, Massachusetts, on 7 October. It became one of the most tragic events of the famine.

Among the crowd assembled at Galway docks on the morning of 7 September waiting patiently to board this ill-fated ship, were Patrick and Mary Sweeney and their eleven children from Lettercallow in Connemara. Others included Honora Burke and her three children and Honora Cullen, who also had three children. A fourteen-year-old boy lurked among the travellers and supplies being prepared for loading onto the ship. He did not have the money for the passage and was awaiting his chance to slip on board, as he had two sisters travelling on the *St. John* and was determined not to be left behind in Galway. Another passenger, Peggy Mullen, was taking her sister's little daughter with her for a fresh start in the New World. The baby's mother had travelled to America on an earlier voyage and was now anxiously awaiting their arrival in Boston. The Egan family – father, mother and child – from County Clare joined the others at the docks. There was a large gathering from County Clare, with people from Connemara and Galway making up the remainder of the passengers. The two-masted brig was manned by a crew of sixteen that day. There was much anguish and many tears as friends and family members crowded the dockside to say farewell to their loved ones. Once the ship was loaded, the passengers, numbering at least 100, made their way up the gangplank and located their bunks.

The rising tide lifted the 200-ton brig, and she was ready to sail. The sailors, supported by the dock crew, cast off, and soon the 90-foot brig began moving out into Galway Bay. There was some excitement among the children as they watched the crew scurrying around the ship, setting the sails in position. As the ship moved out into the bay, passengers watched from the main deck as they sailed past Mutton Island lighthouse and along the coast towards Connemara. The ship anchored at Lettermullen to take on additional passengers and fresh water for the voyage.[9]

Later that same day, the ship sailed out into the Atlantic towards its fate. At first the nervous passengers were huddled together in the cramped steerage quarters, clutching their rosary beads as the ship rose and plunged with the swell of the ocean. Four days into the journey, the stowaway boy was discovered and passed into the care of his sisters. There were days of sunshine and clear skies, and, as passengers became accustomed to the roll of the sea, the journey became more bearable. As the weeks passed there was growing hope of a better life in America. A fiddler played some favourite Irish tunes, giving an air of optimism to the fleeing refugees. The bright sunshine took away much of the sadness, and the ship made good time under favourable winds, adding considerably to the optimism of the passengers. Ireland was soon a lonely and sad distant memory where hunger stalked every road and bótharín.

The *St. John*'s sails billowed in strong winds, and the ship surged forward to the approval of all on board. During the first week of October excitement grew among the passengers as the ship entered the waters of the New World, and many of them lined the gunwales each day to catch their first glimpse of the American coast and their salvation.[10]

The ship made good time, and on Saturday 6 October 1849, the *St. John* entered the waters of Boston Harbour. It had been a good voyage: faster and less hazardous than people had expected for that time of year. The captain gave orders that a ration of 'ardent spirits' be issued to the crew and suggested that the passengers should celebrate their last night on board the *St. John*. The rigging and deck were soon decorated with candles, and plans to spend the night in song and dance were put in place. The passengers had good reason to celebrate: behind them lay a land of starvation, disease and death; ahead of them was a land of golden promise and the hope of a new life.

It was early evening, and light rain began to fall – it may have dampened their bodies but not their spirits, as their new country beckoned just a short distance away. The rain continued to fall and became heavier as the evening wore on, eventually driving the people below deck. The passengers tried to console each other, saying that within a few hours the danger of the sea would be past. However, the faces of the sailors betrayed fear. The weather continued to deteriorate, and by midnight a gale was blowing from the north-east. Howling winds and giant waves surged and crashed against the ship. The terrified passengers were now forced to listen to the sound of the brig's groaning timbers as it fought for survival against the powerful elements. The captain had already issued orders to his crew to lay a course north-east hoping to 'ride out' the fury of the storm, but the brig was taking a serious battering by heavy waves as it pitched and rose in the violent sea. There was no reprieve for the *St. John*; just ahead of it lay the rocks of the Grampus Ledge, feared by all sea captains. The howling storm could not drown out the terrified cries of the passengers below deck as panic spread among them. The more sinister sound from the groaning timbers of the brig continued to unnerve the people as it battled to stay together. Sunday morning arrived with the ship being driven along Massachusetts Bay by the fierce winds. As dawn approached, Captain Oliver realised that he could not 'ride out' the storm and ordered his crew to change course. He was attempting to make a run towards the southern shores of Massachusetts Bay. However, the huge waves forced the brig towards the Cohasset coastline instead. As the captain stared out through the heavy rain and storm, he could see huge white waves smashing against the deadly rocks of Grampus Ledge.[11]

The captain knew that unless his ship could slip past those treacherous rocks they were doomed. Although the sails had already been lowered, the empty masts were swaying back and forth in the violent storm. As there was no way of steering the brig effectively, the captain ordered his crew to drop anchors. There was a rattle of chains, and moments later the anchors touched bottom; there was a shudder as the ship was held in place. It was a desperate gamble. The captain hoped and prayed, as did the others, that the anchors would hold the *St. John* in position until the storm subsided. However, their hope of holding out against the cruel sea was short-lived, and soon the anchors began to drag. The *St. John* lunged forward towards Grampus Ledge as each wall of water drove it closer and closer to the treacherous rocks. Below decks, the terrified people prayed, calling out to God for mercy; some had made their way onto the main deck and were huddled together, terror-stricken, awaiting their fate. They watched with terror-filled eyes as the raging hurricane and gigantic waves carried them closer to doom. In a last desperate attempt to survive, Captain Oliver roared out to his crew to cut the masts, praying that the ferocious wind would have less impact on the ship. The masts with their rigging were cut and fell crashing into the boiling sea, but it was too late. Each breaker was twenty to thirty feet high; then one last huge wave, carrying with it all the fury of the ocean, lifted the stricken ship and smashed it onto the waiting rocks of Grampus Ledge. The initial impact punched a huge hole in the hull, and many of those below deck were drowned within minutes. The *St. John* had no chance against the enormous waves; the helpless ship continued time and again to be smashed against the rocks. The weakened timbers had no chance of holding together against the power of the sea, and it began to break up.[12]

Screaming emigrants and crew rushed forward in an attempt to reach the ship's jollyboat and longboat. Men, women and children clung to the ship's gunwales as the mountainous waves crashed against it, rocking it violently from side to side. The sea snatched many from the heaving deck; these people only stayed afloat for an instant before being swallowed up by the raging waves. The jollyboat sank immediately, leaving the longboat the only chance of salvation, but it had broken loose and was drifting further and further away from the stricken ship. It was certain death for anyone who remained on the sinking vessel, and so the crewmen and many of the passengers leapt into the ferocious sea and thrashed and swam towards the longboat. The sea took all but twelve of the terrified swimmers; the Captain, First Mate, eight crew members and two passengers managed to reach the longboat and clamber into it.

Mary Sweeney and her children were swept to their deaths. Patrick Sweeney grabbed his youngest child, three-year-old Agnes, plunged into the sea clutching his little girl, and struck out, attempting to swim to the longboat. Tragically, moments later, they were struck by a powerful wave, and both father and daughter perished together. Sadly, their fate was shared by most of the emigrants: Peggy Mullen and her sister's baby, and the children of Honora Burke and Honora Cullen were all lost.

When the brig finally split in two, the remaining emigrants were swept into the sea, grasping for any debris that still remained afloat. The wreckage offered some hope of survival, but for most that was all it was, hope, and they succumbed to the sea. A large section of the brig's deck that had split from the ship did stay afloat, resulting in deliverance for some passengers; among them were seven men and two women. They held onto this piece of wreckage and were cast ashore on the Cohasset beach some time later.

There are various accounts of the actual number of people who lost their lives, but a good estimate would be about 140.[13]

The following poem was signed T. F. D. and was written for *The Cork Examiner* in February 1847. It was also published in *The Galway Vindicator*:

RHYMES FOR THE PEOPLE

God of truth! God of love!
Look from thy Throne above,
Down on our misery – down on our woe,

Look with pitying eye,
Down from your home on high!

Mercy, oh God of peace – Thy mercy show!
See our devoted land,
Under gaunt famine's hand,
Trembling – perishing – ready to fall!

List thou our feeble prayer!
God of all Nations hear!
Thou art our only hope – on Thee we call!
Look on the mother wild,
Bowed o'er her famished child
Foodless – half lifeless crushed down with care,
Feeble and faint her sigh,
Death's in her glazed eye,
Broken's her widowed heart – desolate – drear!

See the once stalwart man,
With sunken cheek and wan!
Shrivelled his cheek where was health's ruddy glow,
Hear thou his child's wild cry!
'Bread father! Bread I die!'

Mercy, thy merciful, Thy mercy show!
Look on the damp, cold, bed!
There lies a mother dead!
Look on her infant pale – faint is his cry,
Cry, cry, thy full baby,

Milk there in none for thee,
Her blood in cold, her life's fount is run dry!

Look on the famished throng!
Hear Thou their direful song!
Bread, or we perish – oh give or we die!
On them thy misery shed!
Give them their daily bread,
Oh let a nation's prayers reach Thee on high!

Look on the cabin lone!
Fire on its hearth – there none,
Food neath its ruined roof none is now there,
Life the doomed spot has fled,
Tenanted by the dead,
Shroudless and coffinless – putrid and bare,
There they lie – there they lie,
No, not a mourner's cry,
Sounds through the cheerless home – all are laid low,
Famine its work has done,
Aged and young are gone,
Mercy, oh God of love, Thy mercy show!

Loon on this stricken land!
O'er it, Thy bounteous hand,
Spread God of mercy – oh, spread God of light!
Yield to a people's call,
And let Thy blessings fall,
Full on our native land – plenteous and bright!

Hear thou! oh, hear our cry,

Nor longer let us die,

Perishing – famishing – bowed down with woe!

Peace o'er our island shed!

Now every hope is fled,

Save in Thee, God of love – Thy mercy show![14]

14

IMMIGRANT SOLDIERS

America was the land of hope and salvation for most of the Irish immigrants. However, they faced bigotry in their adopted country as anti-Irish feelings grew. The Irish famine immigrants were the first significant wave of refugees to arrive in the USA.[1] The American authorities in cities such as Boston and New York found themselves overwhelmed by the sheer numbers arriving and were shocked by the scale of their poverty. Some believed that Britain was exporting its problems and responsibilities.

Most of the new arrivals immediately settled into the lowest grade of society and fought a daily battle for survival. Once again they found themselves victims of unscrupulous land-lords as families were packed into totally overcrowded houses. Conditions were brutal, and those with little or no finance were forced to settle in gardens, backyards, alleys and wooden shacks – some worse than the hovels they had left behind in Ireland. Health conditions were extremely poor; there was no privacy and no regard for age or sex, leaving people humiliated and with little sense of decency. They were treated with total indifference and even some hostility, which caused even more despair. In the accommodation close to the dockside warehouses, people lived in musty cellars with low ceilings, some of which would partially flood with the rising tide. For many, the future looked almost as bleak in the new world of 'hope and promise' as it had in the old one of their birth, now ravaged by famine and death.

The Irish immigrants arriving in the USA quickly discovered that they were not welcome. Not only were they the poorest people to arrive on American shores, to make matters worse they were considered the lowest form of human life; their Irish accent, backward style of dress, poverty and illiteracy resulted in their being ridiculed and scorned. They begged in the streets for sustenance, which caused even more resentment towards them. The majority had come from the rural parts of Ireland, and their arrival in American cities was intimidating for them.

However, there was one place where the Irish were welcome, and that was in the army. Some of them became soldiers of note, such as Thomas Francis Meagher, already mentioned; other lesser-known soldiers are profiled below. This chapter will include a sample of these people and the events that shaped their lives and deaths.

The following is an account of Irish emigrants who fled the famine and eventually found themselves fighting in the Mexican-American War of 1846–48. Some of these men initially enlisted in the American army but then deserted and joined the Mexicans. A number of reasons have been suggested as to why this happened, including religious intolerance, alienation, and mistreatment by commanding officers. Others have suggested that the main reason for desertion was a sense of common cultural understanding and ill-treatment experienced by both the Irish and the Mexicans. Some historians also believe that the Irish were attracted by offers from the Mexican government, such as higher wages and generous grants of land. These incentives would have proved very appealing to famine refugees. Regardless of their reasons, deserters would eventually pay an extremely high price for their decision. These men formed the famous San Patricios, later St Patrick's Battalion, led by John O'Reilly from Clifden, County Galway. The San Patricios gave an excellent account of themselves in artillery combat; however, despite this, they were ordered to form part of a larger infantry battalion by General Santa Anna himself. The name of the battalion also changed to the Foreign Legion of Patricios. O'Reilly led the 1st Company while a man named Santiago O'Leary led the 2nd Company. The battalion continued to serve with distinction. It was well known that, if captured, the Irishmen were likely to be executed by the Americans for desertion, and it was alleged that because of this they threatened wavering Mexican troops with death if they retreated during battle.

One of their most famous encounters with American troops was at the Battle of Churubusco on 20 August 1847. The battle centred on the monastery of Churubusco, which resembled a fortress with its imposing stone walls. The San Patricio companies, supported by the Los Bravos Battalion, occupied the monastery. Churubusco became the scene of one of the bloodiest battles of the war. According to some accounts, the soldiers fought under an Irish flag, which O'Reilly described as being a green silk banner with a harp and the motto 'Erin go Bragh'. This was surmounted by the Mexican coat of arms and a motto 'Liberty for the Mexican Republic'. On the other side of the flag was an image of St Patrick holding a key and staff, the latter object holding down a serpent. The defenders fought with tremendous courage and repelled the attacking American forces a number of times. However, they were suffering heavy losses, and when their ammunition began to run out a Mexican officer raised the white flag of surrender. Despite being heavily outnumbered, one of the Irish officers, Captain Patrick Dalton, tore down the white flag. Upon seeing this, the Mexican General, Pedro Anaya, ordered his men to fight on, with their bare hands if necessary. The Mexican historian Heriberto Frías wrote of the heroic last stand of the San Patricios, saying that the brave Irish soldiers of St Patrick defended the Mexican standard with spirited volleys of fire, until the enemy's intensive fire brought death to the valiant marksmen. Once the US forces broke through and breached the Mexican defences, a brutal close-quarter fight took place with bayonets and sabres, but eventually the surviving San Patricios were forced to surrender.

The Irish prisoners were horrifically treated – even worse then the Mexicans – because the Americans saw them as deserters. In addition to this, they had been responsible for some of the toughest fighting and had inflicted some of the heaviest casualties on the American forces. Deserters were defined as those who had defected to the Mexican army after the war broke out. Of the seventy-two men charged with desertion, none of the defendants were accorded a lawyer. Those convicted were hanged, and only a handful faced death by firing squad, which should have been the sentence in all cases, as hanging was reserved for spies and for those who committed atrocities against civilians under the contemporary Articles of War. It is estimated that over 9,000 American soldiers deserted during the Mexican-American War, but it was only the San Patricios who were put to death by hanging. One of the last men to be hanged was Francis O'Connor, and the sentence was carried out even though both his legs had been amputated the previous day.

The Irish soldiers who had changed sides before the war broke out received fifty lashes and were branded with the letter D. They were also forced to wear iron yokes around their necks for the duration of the war. Among their number was John O'Reilly. Although being literally branded as deserters by the Americans, the San Patricios are held in 'everlasting esteem' by the Mexican people and are honoured annually by them. In 1997, President Ernesto Zedillo of Mexico commemorated the 150th anniversary of the execution of the San Patricios at a ceremony in Mexico City's San Jacinto Plaza, where some of the hangings took place. The Irish and Mexican authorities jointly issued commemorative postage stamps to mark the anniversary. This acknowledgement was followed in 2004 by the Mexican government's commissioning of a commemorative statue, which it presented to the Irish government to honour the bravery and sacrifice of the Saint Patrick's Battalion. The statue was erected in Clifden where their leader John O'Reilly was born.[2]

The Irish also fought with distinction on both sides of the American Civil War of 1861–65. The famous 'Fighting' 69th Regiment was noted for its courage in the Union army and won the respect and admiration of the other regiments. It was formed in 1851 by Irish immigrants, many of whom had fled the famine. Among those who were remembered with honour for service during the Civil War was Patrick Kelly from Castlehackett, County Galway. Kelly emigrated to the USA in 1850 and settled in New York. He enlisted as a private in the 69th New York State Militia, and when the American Civil War broke out in 1861 he proved himself an excellent soldier. He quickly rose to the rank of lieutenant, but while he was later promoted to captain with the 16th United States Infantry, he was never actually commissioned. However, he was eventually commissioned a lieutenant colonel with the 88th New York Volunteer Infantry.[3] Kelly was one of the officers who led the Union assault on Marye's Heights at the Battle of Fredericksburg on 13 December 1862. Stonewall Jackson was one of the opposing Confederate commanders. By nightfall, more than 6,000 Union soldiers had perished in the most senseless slaughter of the war. This battle decimated the famed Irish Brigade.[4] A correspondent of *The Times* of London later wrote, 'Never at Fontenoy, Albuera or at Waterloo was more undaunted courage displayed by the sons of Erin.'[5]

On 1 July 1863, the greatest battle ever fought on the North American continent began at Gettysburg. Following the resignation of Union commander General Thomas Francis Meagher, Patrick Kelly was placed in command of the Irish Brigade. The 65,000-strong Confederate army was under the command of Robert E. Lee, and they faced a Union army consisting of some 85,000 men, under General George Meade. With only a fraction of the original command, Kelly led the Irish Brigade into action.[6] On the third day of the battle, 13,000 Confederate troops charged across a mile of ground towards the Irish regiment. Their ranks were decimated as they closed on the Union lines. One of the Confederates killed in the charge was Willie Mitchel, son of the Young Ireland leader John Mitchel.[7] The following day, Robert E. Lee retreated southward, leaving behind 25,000 dead on the battlefield. The Union dead totalled 27,000.[8]

Patrick Kelly was a man of tremendous courage, which possibly led to his being killed while leading his command at the Battle of Petersburg on 16 June 1864. An American newspaper described the scene as Kelly's body was carried from the battlefield, stating that the 'strong old veteran soldiers wept like children, and wrung their hands in a frenzy ... never was there a more unblemished soul in it than honest Colonel Patrick Kelly'.[9] He was forty-three years of age when he was buried at Calvary Cemetery on 26 June 1864.

Another Irish immigrant hero of the American Civil War was Richard 'Dick' Dowling. He was born in 1838, near Tuam in County Galway. Dowling was one of eight children, who, along with their parents, emigrated to New Orleans. In 1853, his parents and four of his siblings died of yellow fever. After this tragedy, Dowling settled in Houston where he married Elizabeth Ann Odlum and established a successful chain of saloons. He enlisted in the Confederate army when the American Civil War broke out. He was part of a Texas battalion composed primarily of Irish dockworkers known as the Jefferson Davis Guards. He served as a lieutenant in the Battle of Galveston in 1863. Following this, Dowling and his company of forty-four Irishmen were assigned to guard an artillery post, Fort Griffin, on the Sabine river. Dowling spent much of his time at this remote outpost instructing his men in artillery training. On 8 September 1863, a Union navy flotilla of 5,000 men attempted to enter the river channel. Dowling's artillery training proved extremely successful, and they scored several direct hits on the flotilla, forcing the Union troops to retreat. They also managed to capture 350 prisoners and a large quantity of supplies; moreover their success prevented the Union invasion of Texas.

The Confederate government honoured Dowling and his men by presenting them with medals inscribed 'Sabine Pass 1864'. Dowling was also personally commended for his leadership by President Jefferson Davis. He subsequently served as a recruiting officer for the Confederacy. After the war he returned to his saloon business in Houston where he was hailed as a hero. He quickly became one of the city's leading businessmen, but his promising future was cut short by an epidemic of yellow fever, and he died on 23 September 1867. In 1905 a statue of Dick Dowling was erected in Houston, and in 1939 it was moved to the Sam Houston Park. It was moved again in 1958 when City Hall was relocated, indicating the importance of this Irish immigrant. In recent years, two memorials were unveiled in Tuam, County Galway: one to Dick Dowling and the other to Patrick Kelly.

It is important to remember that many of the Irishmen who fought on both sides of the American Civil War and, indeed, the wars with the First Nations peoples of that continent, were Irish famine immigrants. However, this is not something we can be proud of, as these native peoples were treated even worse than the Irish themselves.[10] The poem following was written for young men emigrating who found themselves caught up in other conflicts; it was also intended as a reminder that, when trained, it was their duty to return and fight for their own homeland:

THE REBEL BOY

He is gone from the land that he laboured to save,
While a hope of salvation remained,
For a true man was he, and the name of a slave,
To the fell foreign foe he distain'd,
But when union was crushed, and division arose,
And the false found a traitor's employ,
The fate of the freeman in exile he chose,
And left us, the brave Rebel Boy.

And I watched him that day, as he stood on the deck,
Like a high-born chief of the land,
With his green banner bound his bosom and neck,
And his white waving kerchief in hand,
And his eye-beam was bright, and his bearing was proud,
And sweet was the smile of his joy,
As the wild Irish war whoop outburst from the crowd,
For our own gallant brave Rebel Boy.

And his brother was there, and the sisters he loved,
And the parents that in him took pride,
And the maid he adored, whose affection he proved,
And the friend whose good faith he had tried,
And he waved us adieu – while his tear drops did fall,
And sadness o'ershadowed his joy,
And his barque bore him off mid the blessings of all,
On my own gallant brave Rebel Boy.

And he took with him then to his distant exile,

The tale of heart-piercing woes,

That for centuries long, sore affected our Isle,

Neath the ban of her cold-blooded foes,

And his bright sword and pike-head he brought with him too,

And a heart that no bribes could decoy,

And an oath deeply pledged, my loved Erin to you,

By my own gallant brave Rebel Boy.

May God be his speed, for a true man was he,

And determined in heart and in soul,

To tyrants he bent not his neck or the knee,

Nor crouched to alien's control,

But he loved the old land and her foul felon's chain,

He laboured with love to destroy,

But finding alas! that his efforts were vain,

He left us – my brave Rebel Boy.

But he'll come back again when there's virtue abroad,

And liberty leaps from its bier,

When trampled meets trampler, unblenched and unaw'd,

And the faint-hearted fling by their fear,

In his heart's highest hope – in his glory and might,

In the strength of his soul's purest joy,

Then we'll come back again and content for the right,

My true-hearted brave Rebel Boy.[11]

15

THE SILENT PEOPLE

In 1848, Britain declared that the famine was over. This seems somewhat imprudent given that some 1.5 million people were still dependent on charity to survive. Between the years 1848 and 1850 some 500,000 people died, most of them from infectious diseases. Thousands of children were in the care of workhouses, having been either orphaned or abandoned. People were still seeking admission to the workhouses; by then they were known as 'slaughter asylums' as they were no longer being inspected for fear of infection. They had certainly earned this infamous name given that at the beginning of 1848 some 1,460 inmates died in workhouses in one week.[1] This letter to *The Galway Mercury* in November 1849 leaves no doubt as to the situation and who was responsible, and it was also very clear on the solution to Ireland's problems:

> In the opinion of many, the prospect now before our unfortunate countrymen is as gloomy as any season since the commencement of the potato blight – and with such a cheerless vista before them how they will be enabled to drag out a miserable and dreary existence Heaven only knows. The Poor House and the outdoor relief system

are reducing, or have already reduced, to the very verge of almost irremediable pauperism. The Landlords are, with few exceptions, reduced to the level of their pauper tenants; trade, manufactures, commerce, we have none; the entire Nation is now bankrupt. Saxon legislation, the Union with England, and Imperial concentration have reduced Ireland to this, and how else than by ridding ourselves of these three deteriorating agencies we can work out the salvation of Ireland, we are at a loss to determine ... But WE are not in a position to redeem ourselves. We are not in a position to work out regeneration of our sinking country. We are not in a state to enable us to feed our starving poor, and if these are left to the mercy of the Whigs and their rate-in-aid of legislation we shudder to think of the terrible Winter that has already set in upon us, what a terrible Spring awaits us. We are justly alarmed at the reflection that the coming Summer will carry away thousands upon thousands of these poor creatures whom during the last three summers fever and the plague have spared.[2]

By the end of 1850, the worst of the famine was over, and, while there were intervals of blight, the potato was regaining its place as the staple diet of the people. In the years following the famine the survivors were numbed by the tragedy; some research indicates that there was little or no music, singing or dancing in Ireland. These were the 'silent people' so aptly named by the author Walter Macken in the title of his book *The Silent People*, a fictional account of the famine. The whole fabric of society was smashed; the Irish language was almost destroyed as was the tradition of sharing and hospitality. Ireland would never be the same again; many towns and villages were decimated by

A cottage interior, Clare Island.
(*The Illustrated London News*, 1886)

the disaster. Entire communities and villages had disappeared, and thousands of old Irish families had been wiped out or were gone, never to return.[3]

The exodus of Irish people continued, and within twenty years of the famine the population of Ireland was reduced to almost half of what it had been in 1845. Many of those who escaped the famine suffered at the hands of embittered individuals and groups in areas where they sought employment. In 1850, five Irishmen found work labouring in East Riding, Yorkshire. Their work involved reclaiming land from the sea, and they were brought to their place of work by ferry. There was huge resentment among the English labourers, which resulted in a plan to attack the Irishmen when the opportunity arose. It was well planned; they waited until the ferry was at the other side of the harbour before the signal to attack was given. The English workmen then bore down on the Irish with sticks and stones in a violent assault. The victims fled towards the ferry landing area only to realise that it was not there; they immediately plunged into the water in a bid to escape their attackers. They attempted to swim to safety but within minutes they found themselves in trouble. One by one they succumbed and drowned – all but one of them, who managed to reach the opposite shore. There was no apparent remorse among their attackers.[4]

When one considers the anti-Irish racist cartoons which were published in the English magazine *Punch* during the nineteenth century, it is little wonder that Irish people were treated with such bigotry and disdain. Racism has proved a dangerous and frightening scourge over the centuries and has had shocking effects on people right across the world, as, sadly, it continues to do. *Punch* portrayed the Irish as ape-like, pig-like and bestial, as an inferior race of humans. These cartoons bring to mind similar racist images of the Jewish people published by the Nazis before the Second World War, which contributed to the Holocaust.

When a people are deprived of civil rights, civil liberties, religion, education and the ownership of the land of their birth, as was the case in Ireland with the introduction of the penal laws, then the stage is set for disaster. Many harsh judgements and reckless comments were made by people in positions of power in Britain during and before the famine, which certainly did not help the Irish cause. These people neglected to look at the root causes of poverty in Ireland, for which they themselves were responsible. They ignored numerous reports which should have caused alarm bells to ring. There are certain views held throughout Ireland that the famine was allowed to happen to depopulate the country, and it has been described by some people as an Irish holocaust. There are a number of reasons for this school of thought, including the continuation of food exports from Ireland and a lack of adequate government funding. Suffice to say, these issues, along with the similarities between the anti-Irish racist cartoons in *Punch* and anti-Semitic images, give one an idea as to why people would be of this opinion.

In the years following the famine people continued to emigrate, and while the masses gathering in the port towns were greatly reduced, the population was still dwindling, albeit at a slower pace. The 'American Wake' became commonplace, and it was not unusual to see entire families emigrate, although the passengers were mainly young men and women seeking a better future abroad. The pressure was lifted somewhat off the prison system and the workhouses, which returned to some degree of normality. The Sisters of Mercy took over nursing duties at the Galway workhouse in 1865 and took charge of the main section of the workhouse in 1884. The workhouse closed in August 1921, by which time there were only sixty-eight inmates remaining in the complex. They were transferred to the county home in Loughrea, County Galway. The British army occupied the building for a short time before it was handed over to the Irish army in 1922. In 1924, Galway County Council had it converted into the Central Hospital; the last surviving section, the gate lodge, was demolished in 1956. Memories of these dreaded places were passed down through succeeding generations, and a fear of ending one's days in a county home caused much stress among older people, regardless of how well those places were managed.[5] People were also burdened by the memory of the abject poverty of their forefathers, and, over time, the Irish people developed an inbuilt ambition to own the land on which they lived.

Anti-Irish feelings abroad also changed as the immigrants and the descendants of those impoverished Irish people began to prove their outstanding ability to survive, work hard and make a serious impact and contribution in all aspects of life in their adopted countries. They overcame all the obstacles placed before them, and it is a testament to their powerful spirit and endurance that so many of Irish extraction reached the top levels of society in America. It has been estimated that some 40 million people living in the USA today claim Irish ancestry. Many of them maintain that their ancestors arrived there during famine times. Immigrants such as Patrick Kennedy, founder of the Kennedy dynasty, sailed from Wexford to the USA in 1849. His grandson, John F. Kennedy, became one of the most famous presidents of the USA and never forgot his Irish ancestry. Another man who had a major impact on the USA was Henry Ford, founder of the automobile industry. In 1847, his father boarded a ship in Cork bound for Quebec and eventually made his way to Detroit. It is a tribute to their ingenuity and resourcefulness that in just over a generation they transformed themselves from penniless paupers – shunned and degraded – into a people not only accepted but actually envied by so many. This can be witnessed on St Patrick's Day, which is now celebrated by so many cultures across the world. This is their legacy to Ireland, and it is fitting that they are not only remembered poignantly but also, more importantly, with pride.[6]

As mentioned already, there is nothing in Irish history that can be compared to the Great Famine for its immediate impact, its legacy of emigration and cultural loss, and for the decline of the Irish language. However, it is comforting to know that the suffering of these people is now being recognised and honoured. There are now Great Famine memorials in many parts of Ireland and indeed in the USA, Canada, Australia and a number of other countries. Since the 150th anniversary in 1995, many more memorials have been added to the inventory. For example, on Sunday 28 June 1998, the people of Boston dedicated their Irish Famine Memorial Park at the corner of School and Washington Streets. This memorial is intended to forever enshrine a timeless tale of tragedy and triumph. It cost $1 million to complete, and, being located in downtown Boston, it is included on the city's 'Freedom Trail'. Over 3 million people visit the memorial annually. A huge Irish Famine Memorial was also constructed in Battery Park City in Lower Manhattan, New York, to mark the 150th anniversary of the disaster. It commands an 'immense presence' with its features of a stone cottage, stone walls and grassy landscape.[7] In Rhode Island, an Irish Famine Memorial Committee was set up to commemorate and ensure a deeper understanding of the effects of the Great Famine on both Ireland and the thousands of immigrants who eventually settled there.[8]

The Ireland Park in Toronto, Canada, honours the Irish immigrants who fled there during the famine and some 38,000 who arrived in that city in 1847. The vast number of immigrants who arrived in the city is staggering considering that the population of Toronto was a mere 20,000 at the time, and caused serious problems for the city authorities. The park is an acknowledgement to a 'destitute people' who overcame unimaginable hardship and suffering, and it is also a dedication to the kindness and generosity of Canadian people. The haunting sculptures were donated by Norma Smurfit in 1997, and the Ireland Park was officially opened on 21 June 2007.[9] In Australia, the Great Irish Famine Monument was erected in the grounds of the Hyde Park Barracks Museum in Sydney. While it was erected to all who suffered during the catastrophe, it has a special significance for over 4,000 orphans who were sent to Australia between 1848 and 1850.[10]

At home in Ireland, famine memorials and parks continue to be erected and opened. The Irish National Famine Memorial under the shadow of Croagh Patrick, County Mayo, is a very poignant sculpture of a coffin ship by John Behan and a reminder of all who fled the country under such terrible circumstances. It was unveiled on 20 July 1997 by Mary Robinson, then President of Ireland. The rigging contains haunting depictions of skeletons, seemingly crying out for help. In 2009, the government of Ireland established a National Famine Commemoration Committee, which was chaired by Éamonn Ó Cuív, then Minister for Community, Rural and Gaeltacht Affairs. The purpose of the committee was to put plans in place for remembrance services and events that would honour the victims of Ireland's greatest tragedy. This resulted in the inauguration of the first National Famine Memorial Day. It was held on 17 May 2009 in Skibbereen and was the culmination of a week-long series of events to commemorate Ireland's great hunger. Skibbereen was chosen because it was one of the worst-affected areas of the famine. There are mass graves containing the remains of between 8,000 and 10,000 famine victims at Abbeystrewry cemetery near Skibbereen, and they are testament to the tragic consequences of the catastrophic failure of the potato crop. A parallel international event also took place in Canada. All public and sporting events in Ireland observed a minute's silence on the day, which coincided with the 100th anniversary of the erection of a huge Celtic cross on Grosse Île near Quebec City. It stands over 40 feet high and commemorates some 7,000 Irish men, women and children who are buried there.[11]

Commemorations continued in the west of Ireland with the official opening of the Great Famine Memorial Park in Galway city. It was unveiled by Councillor Declan McDonnell, then Mayor of Galway, on Sunday 27 September 2009. The park is in two sections: one commemorates all who fled from Ireland during the famine. It is ideally located at Grattan Road, over-looking the bay and the route taken by the coffin ships as they began their terrifying and perilous voyage over a pitiless ocean. One hundred ships serviced the port of Galway between 1845 and 1850, and it is planned to have the names of the vessels recorded on the memorial. As part of the commemoration, a poster recording the names of the ships was also launched in 2009 and was presented to the Heritage Centre in Skibbereen and Galway City Museum.

The second section of the Great Famine Memorial Park, the Celia Griffin Children's Park, was officially opened by a group of local children. This was a very poignant and historic event for Galway: after 160 years, the famine victims were at last acknowledged and honoured. Celia Griffin was the little six-year-old girl mentioned earlier, who died literally of starvation in the streets of Galway in March 1847. She was just one of hundreds of thousands of children who starved and died while food was being exported out of the country. The organisers of the event felt that by honouring Celia in this very appropriate manner they were honouring all the children who died during these terrible times.[12]

The following poem was written by Private Michael Constable, an Irishman in the British army in August 1847. He was a soldier who recognised and sympathised with the suffering all around him, while he was serving with the 49th Regiment in Clifden:

GOD HELP THE POOR!

God help the poor – the starving poor,
Who linger on from day to day,
Who wander forth from door to door,
Beneath the suns effulgent ray;
Whom toil, and want, and dark despair;
And every human ill hath bow'd,
With thorns entwined, and bound with care;
Before the wealthy and the proud.

God help the poor – attend their wants,
And give them work, and give them bread;

See how you weeping mother pants,
Beside her child, now cold and dead!
Your aged father view, whose locks,
O'erhang his worn and furrow'd brow;
Whom his weak wretched offspring shocks,
God help the poor – God speed the plough.

God help the poor, the night is cold,
The wind howls fiercely o'er the moor,
The lambkins long have left the field,
And loud the angry surges roar,
Bread, bread! – give us bread is the cry,
Of the neglected starving poor,
Who roam beneath their native sky,
And beg for food from door to door.

God help the poor – be this the prayer,
Of every fervent Christian long;
No longer the fiend despair,
With haggard want, their woe prolong;
Too much of late their hearts have bow'd,
To deep oppression and to wrong;
And a few have deign'd – the thoughtless crow'd,
To start a sense of shame – in song.

God help the poor, let minstrels sing;
Let every lyre anew be strung;
And then, may charmed music spring,
With grace and freedom from the tongue,

The Bard's high calling then shall be,
Fulfilled – and all his aid be given,
To gain from wealth, poor charity,
And teach the proud to pray to Heaven!

God help the poor, let none withhold,
Their aid in this sad hour of grief;
The rich can give their prayers and gold,
And most can yield a small relief;
For who that breaths, that doth not feel,
A pang to see the man of toil,
Before his fellow creature kneel,
For leave to till his native soil.

God help the poor, for man is man,
Who should 'brothers be, and a that';
One father owns this earthly clan,
Gives equal laws to poor or great;
But man, man's worst and sternest foe,
The works of his Creator mars,
And strives, the will to overthrow,
Of him who made the moon and stars.

God help the poor, poor artisan,
Who lives by toil and labour hard;
Oh! prosper every worthy plan,
Of him, – of hope, and joy debarred;
Of her, who plys the needle long;
By day and night for daily bread,

Till dimly burns life's lamp – once strong,
Then flickering sleeps – for ever dead.

God help the poor, on whom the light,
Of humble genius deigns to smile;
Who walk in learning path aright,
And, Minerva's vale beguile,
Their leisure hours, by picking fruit,
Of splendid growth, from wisdom's tree;
As forth they go in fond pursuit,
Of such – o'er natures flowery lea.

God help the poor of every land,
Who beat the flail – who guide the plough;
Who sow with grain, their native strand,
And proudly roam the mountain brow;
Whom health and sweet contentment own,
However dark their fate may be;
Who pay obedience to the throne,
With zeal, and fond fidelity.

God help the poor, – let famine cry,
At once be hush'd, and heard no more,
Throughout the land where thousands die,
Oh! soon again health restore;
Fill plenty's horn with ripened grain;
With fruit, and all good earthly things,
And, let our prayers be not in vain,
Breath'd unto Thee, thou 'King of Kings'.

God help the poor of every land;
Be this the universal prayer;
Oh! stretch forth thy Almighty hand,
And save thy children from despair;
Dispel the clouds which o'er them ride,
In gloom, and fearful darkness now,
And henceforth be their friend and guide,
God help the poor – 'God speed the plough'.[13]

16

FAR-REACHING EFFECTS

The famine and the evictions which continued in its wake were major contributors to unrest in Ireland and had far-reaching effects on Irish nationalists both at home and abroad. By 1870, only 3 per cent of Irish householders owned the land they occupied. This led to land agitation and the foundation of the Irish National Land League. One of the league's founders, Michael Davitt from County Mayo, was himself a victim of eviction.

Another blight struck in 1879, bringing with it a renewed hunger and further evictions in the west of Ireland. During this outbreak of famine, the Duke of Edinburgh visited areas around the west coast to witness the distress for himself. He also distributed much-needed supplies to the people. Fortunately this famine was neither as severe nor as widespread as in 1845. Nevertheless, the 1880s also saw much hardship and distress in the west of Ireland, in particular on the islands off the coast. One can see this from news reports and in the illustrations from this period. A report in 1886 stated that if one were to draw a line from Derry in the north of the country to Skibbereen in the south, almost all districts west of this line would be suffering

The famine-stricken peasants. Distress in Ireland – the Duke of Edinburgh and the officers of the Irish Relief Squadron visiting the sick off the west coast. (*The Graphic*, 1880)

from chronic misery. Regarding political promises being made to these people, the report stated that the peasantry, in general, could barely keep themselves alive, and cared little for the 'glorious vision' of the Dublin Parliament.

By this time, the rent was usually earned by one or two male family members who travelled to England or Scotland to work for farmers during harvest time. Women and boys also travelled to seek employment, but this was mainly to Ulster. They had little choice, as most of the farms in the west of Ireland were small and not capable of sustaining a family. In Connacht alone, there were some 70,000 holdings of less than fifteen acres, and 20,000 families were living on less than five acres. People felt that even

The Irish Relief Squadron under the Duke of Edinburgh distributing stores from the *HMS Valorous* at Kilkerran. (*The Illustrated London News*, 1880)

nature was against them as much of the land was unsuitable for crops because of boggy conditions. For many, it still proved almost impossible to pay rents and so evictions continued.[1]

However, by this period people were becoming more resolute in their determination to resist eviction. Tenant farmers and labourers had organised themselves politically and were now being supported by the Land League. Many of them were also funded by donations from the victims of the earlier famine now in America. The league organised boycotts against some of the notorious landlords and had its members physically block evictions. The landlord system had, by the late nineteenth century, taken its toll in Ireland, and a change in attitudes was becoming apparent. In 1886, resistance to evictions came to a head near Woodford, County Galway, with the so-called 'Siege of Sanders Fort'. A number of men barricaded themselves into the house of Thomas Sanders, who was to be evicted on the orders of an absentee landlord over a particularly high rent. Although Sanders and his supporters were eventually forced to concede by a large force of troops and police, their resistance was widely publicised and captured the imagination of many tenant farmers who up until then had been easily intimidated.[2]

Constabulary going in 'Hookers' to enforce evictions on islands off the west coast. (*The Illustrated London News*, 1887)

Nationalist reporters used such resistance to their full advantage, and it was also a chance to condemn absentee landlords. One of them, writing for *The Galway Mercury* on 27 March 1847, stated, 'Of all the evils which can afflict a country, scarcely excepting famine and pestilence, that of Absenteeism must be looked upon as the greatest.' He went on to say that the money extracted from the poor of Ireland was used to embellish English parks and gardens.[3] Such statements had the desired effect, causing even more resentment and resistance. However, with regard to the Woodford case, this particular landlord, Hubert George de Burgh Canning, was totally driven by personal greed and later became known as 'Ireland's Meanest Man'. He was an absolute miser who lived in London, and, while he was extremely wealthy, he dressed and ate in such a manner that one would have assumed he was poverty-stricken. He was the cause of much stress for his tenants and would have them evicted if they could not meet his exorbitantly high rents. The landlords, through their indifference and cruelty, were the architects of their own demise.[4]

The only real hope for Ireland, and for repeal of the Union, had been Daniel O'Connell, but he had lost the nerve to follow this path in 1843 having served a prison sentence. While some may criticise O'Connell because of this, it must be remembered that he was a pacifist and was also seriously concerned for the safety of the Irish people. Another reason for his anti-violent views was that he had killed a man in a duel in 1815 and it had affected him throughout his life. Although his efforts to repeal the Union were in vain, O'Connell did give the Irish people hope. He died in 1847 in the blackest year of the famine with his country in total ruins. Many of the people he had tried so hard to help to raise their living standards were starving and destitute. The great 'Liberator' was dead, and so, it seemed, was any hope for Ireland. The following extract was published in tribute to O'Connell's pacifist views:

Yet, bloodless was his great and grand career;

The sword of slaughter shuddering still to wield;

He spar'd the widow's wail, the orphan's tear,

The purpled horrors of the battle field;

But when to moral force did despots yield?

With such in vain shall right or justice plead;

Valour alone will prove a nation's shield;

Let none then preach the coward's dastard creed;

Save those whose craven hearts would shrink and fear to bleed.[5]

Other means of liberation would have to be explored by a new breed of nationalists. The aftermath of the famine left bitter resentment towards England and led to many nationalist organisations being founded. Some were interested in reviving Irish traditions and culture and in giving Irish people a renewed pride in their heritage. However, others were more volatile, and their aims were to support total separation from England.

On St Patrick's Day 1858 the Irish Republican Brotherhood was founded by James Stephens in Dublin. The Brotherhood was pledged to Irish independence – and to achieve it by physical force if necessary. From its foundation, the Brotherhood supported every organisation with separatist ideals. It survived for many years with financial support from the Fenian movement in America. Many of these people were the survivors and children of the survivors of the famine. They believed that it was now 'payback time' for the forced emigration of countless thousands, who carried with them a deep animosity towards England.[6] One of the most renowned Fenians of the period was Jeremiah O'Donovan Rossa. He had witnessed his own family's departure for the USA during the famine and never forgot that heartbreaking day as he watched them 'weeping and wailing' making their way along the road from Skibbereen.[7] O'Donovan Rossa later emigrated to the USA and became one of the leading figures of the Fenian movement.[8]

The Nation newspaper also played a part in the fight for justice. The founders of *The Nation* were Thomas Davis, John Blake Dillon and Charles Gavan Duffy. It was an important publication during the nineteenth century as it attracted and connected many Irish nationalists. One of its prolific writers and poets was Mary Anne Kelly, more commonly known as 'Eva of *The Nation*'. She was born *circa* 1830, near Headford, County Galway. At the tender age of fourteen she began writing for the newspaper. She became one of the most talented of a group of young people, who during the 1840s set themselves the task of reawakening the spirit of a depressed and downcast nation. Kelly's writings were almost as eagerly welcomed by the readers of *The Nation* as were her poems, which had their source in a heart full of love for Ireland and its people. Although she was gentle by nature, she was a passionate nationalist who expressed her opinions in the strongest possible manner. Her ultimate objective for Ireland was the setting up of a national independent state, free from outside imperial domination, a state that pledged civil rights for its entire people. Through her literary talent she managed to inspire a generation of 'Young Irelanders' during the nineteenth century. Although Kelly's work would not be considered sophisticated, one should bear in mind that it was written with passion and enthusiasm rather than with a stylish hand. She expressed her emotions and political convictions totally and was absolutely convinced that the aims of the nationalists were achievable. She was very aware of her own Irish heritage, believing that she was descended from the O'Kelly clan, lords of Ui Maine, on her father's side and, on her mother's side from the legendary Grace O'Malley. Her grand-uncle, Francis O'Flaherty, was a member of the United Irishmen and had been involved in the 1798 Rebellion.[9]

In support of Daniel O'Connell, Eva requested through her readership that all political parties should unite and work towards the Repeal of the Union. Thomas Davis was one of Kelly's greatest inspirations. She was extremely shocked and saddened by his premature death from scarlet fever in the autumn of 1845 as the famine began to creep across the country.[10] The onslaught of the famine and its eventual outcome reinforced her belief in the need for Irish independence.

Kelly's admiration for the leaders of the Young Ireland movement is certainly displayed in her poetry. In particular, Thomas Francis Meagher, John Mitchel and William Smith O'Brien are prominent in her writing. She knew these men well, and her work for *The Nation* was clearly influenced by them. She dedicated a number of poems to Thomas Francis Meagher following the failed rebellion of 1848. In May 1849, following the commuting of the death sentence of William Smith O'Brien to transportation, Kelly went to visit him and presented him with a small book of twelve poems, which she had just published. Her future husband, Kevin Izod O'Doherty, another committed nationalist, was also transported because of his political views. Although he gave her freedom to move on with her life, she refused and awaited his return to marry him. They eventually ended up in Australia, where both of them died in virtual poverty. They were buried in Brisbane Cemetery where a Celtic cross was erected over their grave.[11]

Even by present-day standards, Kelly would be considered an incredible woman, but by nineteenth-century standards she could be considered extraordinary. She was a pure romantic, with a deep love and passion for her country. The sights that she witnessed during the famine stayed with her all her life, and her poetry most certainly set the hearts of young nationalists ablaze with the ideals of independence. She also paved the way for women to take a more active role in Irish affairs.[12] The poem included at the end of this chapter is a sample of her work.

Another organisation that helped develop a sense of pride in being Irish was the Gaelic Athletic Association (GAA). It was founded on 1 November 1884 by Michael Cusack and a number of others in Thurles, County Tipperary. It quickly connected communities and built strong and lasting comradeship among the various parishes. Cusack himself said that the GAA swept across the country like a prairie fire and he believed that every parish in the country was fielding hurling and football teams within a short time. Handball and camogie became part of the overall sporting structure of the GAA as they began to organise competitions for these games also. Because the GAA was a sporting organisation, it had the added advantage of influencing young people. The games drew huge crowds from the beginning, and, without realising it, the GAA had set in motion a social revolution. Many of its founding fathers were survivors of the famine, who were now using the ancient sports of Ireland to instil a sense of pride in the Irish.

People have often questioned the ban which was introduced prohibiting members of the Royal Irish Constabulary (RIC) from joining the organisation. The GAA have been criticised because of this, but given the spate of evictions and the hardships suffered by the people under the established rule of the day, it is understandable. One must also take into consideration that this ban was introduced at a time when most evictions took place in the presence of the RIC, who were present in case there was any resistance. The GAA was founded at a vital time in Ireland's history as it revived the traditional games and gave the youth of the country a strong connection with the past and provided them with a healthy lifestyle of sport, competition, friendship and a powerful belief in themselves, which has continued to present times.[13]

In 1893 the Gaelic League was founded by Fr Eugene O'Growney, Eoin MacNeill and Douglas Hyde, who later became the first president of Ireland. The purpose of the league was to revive the Irish language, music, dancing, poetry, literature and history. The Gaelic League quickly spread throughout the country, and eventually about 600 branches were established. Many of the people who populated the League had strong memories of the famine and even stronger nationalistic views. Its members were also encouraged to use only Irish manufactured goods, and the league would not award prizes at an Oireachtas, an Irish music and dancing competition, unless the competitors could guarantee that they were dressed in costumes made from Irish materials.[14]

Ironically, one of the main figures behind the collecting and revival of Irish legends at this time was Lady Isabella

Augusta (Persse) Gregory of Roxborough House, County Galway. Her family were of the Protestant landed gentry class and were prominent unionists. At the age of twenty-eight she had married widower Sir William Gregory of Coole, who was thirty-five years her senior. In 1896 William Butler Yeats and Arthur Symons visited Edward Martyn at Tulira Castle in County Galway, where they met Lady Gregory for the first time. This meeting led to the seeds of the Irish Literary Theatre being sown. Lady Gregory collected folklore stories from local people living around the countryside, and through this medium she gained a comprehensive knowledge of the famine. She supported a host of Irish writers and artists from that period until her death in 1932. Through her actions, she redeemed some respect for the landed gentry with regard to the memories of the famine. Her understanding of the native Irish culture led to her making the following statement: 'I defy anyone to study Irish history without getting a dislike and distrust of England.'[15] She also redeemed her married name to some extent, and, as a result, some people began to accept that the infamous 'Gregory Clause' was a serious error in judgment, rather than a deliberate attempt to withhold relief from those who needed it.

The 1903 Wyndham Act allowed most Irish tenants to purchase their holdings from the landlords with the assistance of the British government. The landlords received a generous sum for their property, which was set by the government, while the tenants would repay the government over time. This ultimately resulted in the demise of a centuries-old landlord system and the exploitation of the Irish people.[16]

On the political side, Isaac Butt founded the Home Rule League in 1870. Charles Stewart Parnell took over the leadership of the Irish Parliamentary Party in 1879 and responsibility for the Home Rule campaign. This issue dominated Irish affairs for many years and whether or not it would be implemented was the burning question in Irish politics until the First World War began in 1914. The new leader of the Irish Parliamentary Party, John Redmond, supported England's war effort against Germany. The war changed everything and split the Irish Volunteer Force, a paramilitary movement which had been founded in 1913 to reinforce the political movement for Home Rule, with the vast majority of its members following Redmond. These men found themselves fighting a brutal war for the 'freedom of small nations'.

The Home Rule Bill was suspended because of the European conflict, and some Irish nationalists, fearing that it would never be implemented, decided on more dissident means of gaining independence. History and famine had taught them not to trust the parliament in Westminster, and many of them felt that the time was right to strike at the very heart of the British Empire. With the financial support from descendants of the famine victims in the USA, they decided on an uprising. On 24 May 1916, rebellion broke out in Dublin, with the main buildings in the capital being occupied by the rebels. Most of the seven leaders took over the General Post Office and made it their headquarters. One of the rebels in that building was Michael Collins from west Cork, who grew up listening to stories of the famine; 'revenge for Skibbereen' was now at hand.

The rising continued for one bloody week until the insurgents were forced to surrender. While the rebellion was frowned upon by the majority of Irish people at the time, the execution of its leaders changed the whole course of Irish history. The years following the rebellion saw a new and more volatile force arise: the Irish Republican Army. It was inevitable that violence would erupt, and it did in 1919 with the beginning of the War of Independence. This war ultimately led to the signing of the Anglo-Irish Treaty and the foundation of the Free State in 1922.[17]

Most of the land on which the people of the famine had toiled was at last in Irish hands. The land had always been precious to the Irish people and without its 'fruit' they had died. Another people who held the land sacred and who recognised the suffering of the Irish during the famine were the Choctaw First Nation people of America. They had financially supported the Irish people during their time of need. The First Nation people were no strangers to suffering themselves because of their beliefs and their protection of the land. They believed that the suffering of the Irish people reflected their own plight. John Wooden Legs of the Cheyenne once said, 'Our land is everything to us ... I will tell you one of the things we remember of our land. We remember that our grandfathers paid for it – with their lives.' This quote was recorded over 100 years ago, and it had as much meaning to the Irish as to the indigenous people of America. This had also been true of the Irish people over the centuries, but more died in that horrific five years of famine than ever before. That tragedy has left an inbuilt desire among the Irish to own the land upon which they work and the homes in which they live.

Referring to the emigration from Ireland, an American newspaper reporter wrote shortly after the famine that within a few years a 'Celtic Irishman' will be as rare in Connemara as a 'Red Indian on the shores of Manhattan'.[18] Thankfully this prediction did not materialise, and the Irish language is still spoken in parts of Connemara. As you travel through this beautiful countryside today you cannot even begin to imagine the horrors which the land has witnessed. However, there are poignant reminders of the famine still dotting the landscape: the ruined old deserted houses and villages, and, on some hillsides, the remains of potato ridges, reminders of an unfortunate and silent people long since gone but thankfully not forgotten.

A Cry from the Land

Stand calmly if you will,
Mid a hideous wreck,
T'at makes the storm nerves thrill,
And the heart grow sick,
Let not a murmur breathe,
Of ought that throbs breath,
But, by the might of Death!
I say – Remember!

Let thousands writhe and grasp,
Every day and hour,
In the cold ruthless grasp,
Of the famine – power,

Let madness, rage, despair,
Each heart lay waste and bare,
But hear at last this prayer,
Of mine – Remember!

Crouch lower 'neath the heel,
Of your master's yet,
Be silent while the seal,
On your brows is set,
Nor word nor blow – cold slaves!
But your father's grave,
By him who strikes or saves,
You must – Remember!

Oh ye of fiery words,
Which have shown their worth,
Men of sheathed swords,
Now the scorn of earth!
Still, still for ev'n ye,
One duty learn to see,
Tho' shatter'd all may be,
It is – Remember!

There's a shame more burning still,
Ev'n than that you bear,
There's a course more dread and fell,
Than has fall'n beware!
And oh, that curse and shame,
Would scorch the hellish flame,

If e'er oblivion came,
Then – then – Remember!

Deep, deep within your breast,
Hold each memory dire,
As a sanctified bequest,
Aye, to son from sire,
Let those thoughts grow still and deep,
Till they burst one day from sleep,
And like a whirlwind sweep,
O, men – Remember!

Dare – dare not betray,
This most precious trust,
Till life's breath pass away,
Guard it well ye must,
Like thunder-peal o'erhead,
A voice comes loud and dread,
To waken ev'n the dead,
It says – Remember!

Yes tho' centuries have pass'd,
Yet the stranger still,
Is a stranger to the last,
And so ever will,
A sacred wall of heat,
Stands twixt us strong as fate,
What hand may dare prostrate,
That bar? – Remember!

By them, the faithful few,
With 'traitor' brand,
Who 'thought the wrought' for you,
With devotion grand,
By this wild, woeful night,
That shows no gleam of light,
By all those hopes so bright,
Now quenched – Remember?[19]

NOTES

INTRODUCTION

1. W. Henry, *Coffin Ship: The Wreck of the Brig St. John*, Cork: Mercier Press, 2009, p. 79.

1 PATH TO HUNGER

1. C. Woodham-Smith, *The Great Hunger*, New York: Harper & Row, 1991, pp. 15–16.
2. *Ibid.*, p. 17.
3. C. Kerrigan, 'Temperance and Politics in Pre-Famine Galway', *Journal of the Galway Archaeological and Historical Society*, 43 (1991), pp. 87, 89.
4. Woodham-Smith, *The Great Hunger*, pp. 17–18.
5. *Ibid.*, p. 18.
6. *Ibid.*, pp. 18–19.
7. M. Langan-Egan, 'Some Aspects of the Great Famine in Galway', *Journal of the Galway Archaeological and Historical Society*, 51 (1999), pp. 122–3.
8. Woodham-Smith, *The Great Hunger*, p. 22.
9. H. Litton, *The Irish Famine: An Illustrated History*, Dublin: Wolfhound Press, 1994, p. 12.
10. P. O'Dowd, *The Great Famine and the West, 1845–1850*, Galway: Galway City Council, 1995, pp. 3, 23.
11. Woodham-Smith, *The Great Hunger,* pp. 3, 22–3.
12. W. Henry, *Role of Honour: Mayors of Galway City, 1485–2001*, Galway: Galway City Council, 2001, p. 93.
13. Litton, *The Irish Famine*, p. 10.

14. O'Dowd, *The Great Famine and the West*, p. 3.

15. Litton, *The Irish Famine*, p. 15.

16. Woodham-Smith, *The Great Hunger*, p. 25.

17. Litton, *The Irish Famine*, p. 15.

18. Woodham-Smith, *The Great Hunger*, pp. 29–33.

19. 'The Irish Labourers' *Pater Nostre*', *The Galway Mercury*, 16 January 1847.

2 THE BLIGHT APPEARS

1. Woodham-Smith, *The Great Hunger*, p. 36.

2. Litton, *The Irish Famine*, p. 13.

3. Woodham-Smith, *The Great Hunger*, p. 24.

4. 'The Devon Commission', *The Galway Mercury*, 26 June 1847.

5. Woodham-Smith, *The Great Hunger*, p. 21.

6. Litton, *The Irish Famine*, p. 17.

7. B. Ó Cathaoir, *Famine Diary*, Dublin: Irish Academic Press, 1999, pp. 3–4.

8. Woodham-Smith, *The Great Hunger*, p. 48.

9. 'The Potato Crop', *The Galway Mercury*, 25 October 1845.

10. Ó Cathaoir, *Famine Diary*, p. 5.

11. Litton, *The Irish Famine*, p. 24.

12. *Ibid.*

13. Woodham-Smith, *The Great Hunger*, p. 57.

14. Litton, *The Irish Famine*, pp. 25, 29.

15. The Reformation Online, 'The Great Irish Famine (1846–52), http://www.reformation.org/irish_famine.html (accessed May 2009).

16. Litton, *The Irish Famine*, pp. 29–30.

17. W. Henry, *St Clerans: The Tale of a Manor House*, Galway: Merv Griffin, 1999, pp. 13–14.

18. 'The Curse of the Whigs', *The Galway Vindicator*, 17 April 1847.

3 WORST FEARS REALISED

1. Litton, *The Irish Famine*, pp. 36–9.
2. Woodham-Smith, *The Great Hunger*, p. 89.
3. Litton, *The Irish Famine*, pp. 45–6.
4. Henry, *Coffin Ship*, p. 78.
5. Litton, *The Irish Famine*, p. 46.
6. Henry, *Coffin Ship*, p. 69.
7. Langan-Egan, 'Some Aspects of the Great Famine in Galway', p. 132.
8. Litton, *The Irish Famine*, p. 46.
9. 'Starvation – Inquest', *The Galway Vindicator*, 13 March 1847.
10. Litton, *The Irish Famine*, p. 49.
11. 'Murder in Costello', *The Galway Mercury*, 10 October 1847.
12. P. Ó Laoi, '1847: Famine in Galway', *Galway Roots/Clanna na Gaillimhe*, 3 (1996), pp. 17–19.
13. 'The Great Famine's Effect on Galway', *Galway Independent*, 29 July 2009.
14. Litton, *The Irish Famine*, p. 55.
15. Langan-Egan, 'Some Aspects of the Great Famine in Galway', p. 129.
16. Litton, *The Irish Famine*, pp. 57–65.
17. Ó Cathaoir, *Famine Diary*, p. 168.
18. 'An Unseemly Brawl over God and Scripture', *Galway Advertiser*, 13 November 2008.
19. Litton, *The Irish Famine*, p. 66.
20. 'The Poor Man's Harvest: A Dirge', *The Galway Vindicator*, 13 October 1847.

4 FAMINE STRIKES GALWAY

1. J. P. Murray, 'The Great Famine in Galway', *Galway Roots/Clanna na Gaillimhe*, 3 (1996), p. 1.
2. Henry, *Coffin Ship*, pp. 25–7.

3. Ó Cathaoir, *Famine Diary*, p. 7.

4. *Ibid.*, p. 39.

5. P. O'Dowd, *Old and New Galway*, Galway: The Archaeological, Historical and Folklore Society, Regional Technical College, Galway, and The Connacht Tribune Ltd, 1985, p. 31.

6. 'Notice', *The Galway Mercury*, 24 January 1846.

7. Henry, *Coffin Ship*, pp. 70–2.

8. Murray, 'The Great Famine in Galway', p. 1.

9. 'More Deaths by Starvation', *The Galway Mercury*, 22 January 1848.

10. 'Galway Union: State of the House', *The Galway Vindicator*, 15 May 1850.

11. 'Starvation', *The Galway Mercury*, 16 January 1847.

12. Ó Cathaoir, *Famine Diary*, p. 48.

13. Henry, *Coffin Ship*, pp. 70–2.

14. Ó Laoi, '1847: Famine in Galway', p. 17.

15. O'Dowd, *Old and New Galway*, pp. 73–7.

16. S. McGuire, 'Famine Relief', *Galway Reader*, 3 (1–2) (1950), pp. 71–2.

17. Ó Laoi, '1847: Famine in Galway', pp. 17–18.

18. *Ibid.*

19. 'Steaming Along', *Galway Advertiser*, 14 May 1992.

20. Ó Cathaoir, *Famine Diary*, p. 34.

21. 'Distress in the West', *The Galway Mercury*, 13 June 1847.

22. 'Outrage', *The Galway Vindicator*, 18 December 1847.

23. Ó Cathaoir, *Famine Diary*, p. 60.

24. Ó Laoi, '1847: Famine in Galway', pp. 17–18.

25. 'Claddagh Relief Establishment', *The Galway Mercury*, 30 January 1847.

26. Murray, 'The Great Famine in Galway', p. 1.

27. 'Widows and Orphans Asylum', *The Galway Mercury*, 22 January 1848.

28. 'The Poor Man's Christmas: A Carol for the Year of Famine', *The Galway Mercury*, 2 January 1847.

5　A BRUTAL WINTER

1. 'Town Commissioners', *The Galway Vindicator*, 4 September 1847.

2. O'Dowd, *Old and New Galway*, p. 59.

3. 'Nuns' Island Whiskey', *Galway Advertiser*, 6 August 2009.

4. 'Galway Industrial Society', *The Galway Vindicator*, 23 June 1847.

5. Murray, 'The Great Famine in Galway', pp. 1–2.

6. Ó Cathaoir, *Famine Diary*, p. 68.

7. *Ibid.*, p. 84.

8. G. Garvey, *Bushypark Celebrates 1837–1987*, Bushypark, Galway: Fr Gerard Garvey, 1988, p. 8.

9. 'Additional Poor House', *The Galway Vindicator*, 9 February 1848.

10. Murray, 'The Great Famine in Galway', pp. 1–2.

11. Henry, *Coffin Ship*, pp. 70–2.

12. 'More Deaths by Starvation', *The Galway Mercury*, 23 January 1847.

13. 'Starvation', *The Galway Mercury*, 16 January 1847.

14. 'Spread of Fever', *The Galway Mercury*, 20 May 1847.

15. Langan-Egan, 'Some Aspects of the Great Famine in Galway', pp. 128–9.

16. 'The Potato Crop', *The Galway Mercury*, 25 October 1845.

17. Langan-Egan, 'Some Aspects of the Great Famine in Galway', pp. 128–9.

18. 'Randolph Routh + 1858' available online at http://genealogy. links.org/linkscgi/readged?home/ben/camilla-genealogy/current +c-routh88898+2-2-0-1-0 (accessed May 2009).

19. Oxford Companion to Irish History, 'Gregory Clause', available online at http://www.encyclopedia.com/doc/1O245-Gregoryclause. html (accessed May 2009).

20. Ó Cathaoir, *Famine Diary*, pp. 124–45.

21. 'Extermination', *The Galway Vindicator*, 23 September 1848.

22. 'Gregory's Quarter Acre', *The Galway Mercury*, 27 January 1849.

6 STARVATION WITNESSED

1. 'A Famine Report', *The Galway Mercury*, 13 March 1847.
2. Ó Cathaoir, *Famine Diary*, p. 92.
3. 'A Famine Report'.
4. Ó Cathaoir, *Famine Diary*, p. 119.
5. 'More Deaths by Starvation', *The Galway Mercury*, 23 January 1847.
6. 'A Famine Report'.
7. 'More Deaths by Starvation'.
8. *Ibid.*
9. Ó Cathaoir, *Famine Diary*, p. 99.
10. *Ibid.*, p. 91.
11. *Ibid.*, p. 145.
12. 'Claddagh Relief Establishment', *The Galway Mercury*, 30 January 1847.
13. 'A Famine Report'.
14. 'Herring Fishery', *The Galway Vindicator*, 15 September 1847.
15. 'A Famine Report'.
16. 'The Famine Stricken', *The Galway Mercury*, 13 February 1847.

7 BLACK FORTY-SEVEN

1. 'We are Starving, Bread or Employment', *The Galway Vindicator*, 8 May 1847.
2. Ó Cathaoir, *Famine Diary*, p. 119.
3. Ó Laoi, '1847: Famine in Galway', p. 18.
4. 'Starvation – Inquest', *The Galway Vindicator*, 13 March 1847.
5. Murray, 'The Great Famine in Galway', p. 3.
6. 'Fever in Galway', *The Galway Vindicator*, 23 October 1847.
7. 'Mortality amongst the Gentry', *The Galway Mercury*, 1 May 1847.
8. 'Death of Marcus Lynch', *The Galway Vindicator*, 29 January 1848.
9. Murray, 'The Great Famine in Galway', p. 3. The British Relief Association had been active in its support from the outset of the famine but found it extremely difficult to deal with the situation as it continued.

10. 'Another Victim among the Clergy: Death of the Rev. J. Roche RCC', *The Galway Vindicator*, 4 September 1847.

11. 'Want of Burial Ground', *The Galway Vindicator*, 2 June 1847.

12. P. Ó Laoi, 'Famine in Castlegar', *Galway Roots/Clanna na Gaillimhe*, 3 (1996), pp. 59–60.

13. 'State of the People', *The Galway Vindicator*, 31 March 1847.

14. 'Irish Sufferings: Whig and Tory Sympathy', *The Galway Mercury*, 3 July 1847.

15. Bicentenary Committee, *By the Narrow Gate: A Bicentenary History*, Galway: Bicentenary Committee, 2008, p. 25.

16. 'Orphan's Breakfast Institute', *The Galway Mercury*, 31 July 1847.

17. *Ibid.*

18. *Ibid.*

19. A. MacLochlainn and T. Regan, 'The Claddagh Piscatory School', in *Two Galway Schools*, Galway: Galway Labour History Group, 1993, pp. 14–15.

20. P. O'Dowd, *Down by the Claddagh*, Galway: Kenny's Bookshop and Art Galleries Ltd, 1993, pp. 43–4.

21. 'Claddagh Piscatory School', *The Galway Vindicator*, 29 September 1847.

22. O'Dowd, *Down by the Claddagh*, p. 43.

23. S. McGuire, 'Education: Galway Grammar School', *Galway Reader*, 3 (1–2) (1950), pp. 56–8.

24. O'Dowd, *Down by the Claddagh*, p. 19.

25. Ó Laoi, '1847 – Famine in Galway', p. 19.

26. 'Irish Sufferings: Whig and Tory Sympathy', *The Galway Mercury*, 3 July 1847.

27. 'American Relief for Galway', *The Galway Vindicator*, 21 July 1847.

28. Ó Laoi, 'The Famine in Castlegar', p. 60.

29. Murray, 'The Great Famine in Galway', p. 2.

30. 'Food Riots', *The Galway Vindicator*, 6 October 1847.

31. Ó Laoi, 'The Famine in Castlegar', p. 60.

32. 'Food Riots'.

33. Ó Cathaoir, *Famine Diary*, p. 156.

34. *Ibid.*, pp. 157.

35. 'Assistant Chaplain to the Workhouse', *The Galway Vindicator*, 27 November 1847.

36. 'Extermination: The Court of Chancery', *The Galway Mercury*, 30 October 1847.

37. 'Frightful Influx of Evicted Cottier Paupers', *The Galway Vindicator*, 18 December 1847.

38. 'The Society of Friends', *The Galway Vindicator*, 20 October 1847.

39. 'Frightful Influx of Evicted Cottier Paupers'.

40. 'A Lay of Sorrow', *The Galway Mercury*, 20 February 1847.

8 ANOTHER YEAR OF SADNESS

1. 'State of the Town', *The Galway Mercury*, 29 January 1848.

2. 'More Deaths by Starvation', *The Galway Mercury*, 22 January 1848.

3. 'State of the Town'.

4. 'Notice to Paupers Receiving Outdoor Relief', *The Galway Mercury*, 22 January 1848.

5. Henry, *Coffin Ship*, pp. 70–1.

6. 'More Deaths by Starvation'.

7. Henry, *Coffin Ship*, pp. 42–3.

8. *Ibid.*, pp. 44–6.

9. Ó Cathaoir, *Famine Diary*, p. 104.

10. 'Irish Extermination', *The Galway Vindicator*, 8 April 1848.

11. Ó Laoi, 'The Famine in Castlegar', p. 60.

12. Ó Cathaoir, *Famine Diary*, p. 162.

13. 'Extermination in the County', *The Galway Mercury*, 17 June 1848.

14. Ó Cathaoir, *Famine Diary*, p. 164.

15. Murray, 'The Great Famine in Galway', p. 3.

16. 'More Evictions', *The Galway Vindicator*, 5 July 1848.

17. P. O'Dowd, *Galway City Waterways: A Walking Tour*, Galway: Peadar O'Dowd, 1985, p. 11.

18. M. Semple, *Reflections on Lough Corrib*, Galway: Maurice Semple, 1974, pp. 7–19.

19. K. Villiers-Tuthill, 'The Clifden Union', *Galway Roots/Clanna na Gaillimhe*, 3 (1996), pp. 6–7.

20. 'Miserable Conditions of the Poor in Galway', *The Galway Vindicator*, 1 December 1848.

21. 'Lament of the Ejected Irish Peasant', *The Galway Mercury*, 12 January 1850.

9   WILL HUNGER EVER END?

1. 'The Irish Fisheries', *The Galway Vindicator*, 2 October 1849.

2. 'Deep Sea Fishery', *The Galway Vindicator*, 11 July 1849.

3. 'Galway Herring Fishery', *The Galway Vindicator*, 24 August 1850.

4. 'Claddagh Curing House', *The Galway Vindicator*, 13 January 1849.

5. 'A Claddagh Fisherman', *The Galway Vindicator*, 24 March 1849.

6. O'Dowd, *Down by the Claddagh*, pp. 16–17.

7. 'Death of the Admiral of the Claddagh Fishermen', *The Galway Vindicator*, 28 April 1849.

8. 'Sketches of Ireland', *The Illustrated London News*, 16 July 1870.

9. 'Destitution in Galway', *The Galway Vindicator*, 10 February 1849.

10. 'Frightful Destitution in Mayo', *The Galway Vindicator*, 17 February 1849.

11. 'The Working of the Poor Law', *The Galway Vindicator*, 10 March 1849.

12. *Ibid.*

13. *Ibid.*

14. 'Galway Union: State of the House', *The Galway Mercury*, 24 March 1849.

15. Ó Cathaoir, *Famine Diary*, p. 166.

16. Langan-Egan, 'Some Aspects of the Great Famine in Galway', pp. 127–8.

17. L. H. Walker, *One Man's Famine*, Galway: Centenary Committee,

1978, pp. 92–3.

18. 'State of the Town and of the Prisons', *The Galway Vindicator*, 28 February 1849.

19. 'A Few Days', *The Galway Vindicator*, 27 January 1849.

20. 'State of the County and Town Prison', *The Galway Vindicator*, 10 February 1849.

21. *Ibid.*

22. 'Two Deaths from the effects of Starvation', *The Galway Vindicator*, 28 February 1849.

10   UNRELENTING SUFFERING

1. 'Deaths from Starvation', *The Galway Vindicator*, 14 February 1849.

2. 'Awful Mortality in the Ballinasloe Workhouses', *The Galway Vindicator*, 12 May 1849.

3. 'Decrease of the Population', *The Galway Vindicator*, 31 October 1849.

4. 'The Process of Slow Poisoning: Diet of the "Mere Irish" Pauper', *The Galway Vindicator*, 12 May 1849.

5. 'The Commissariat', *The Galway Mercury*, 13 May 1848.

6. *Ibid.*

7. Walker, *One Man's Famine*, p. 72.

8. 'Letter to the Editor', *The Tablet*, 23 May 1848.

9. 'Death of Major M'Kie', *The Galway Vindicator*, 20 June 1849.

10. 'Just Found Out: Horrible Oh! Horrible', *The Galway Mercury*, 18 March 1848.

11. 'Unsound Food', *The Galway Mercury*, 29 July 1848.

12. P. O'Dowd, 'The Famine: Think About It!' *St Patrick's Parish Christmas Magazine* (1995), pp. 21–2.

13. J. Casserly, *An Open Door: A History of the St Vincent de Paul Society, 1849–1999*, Galway: St Vincent de Paul Society, 1999, p. 1.

14. 'Evictions of Householders in Galway', *The Galway Vindicator*, 30 January 1850.

15. 'Committals to Our County Prison: State of the Country', *The Galway Vindicator*, 17 July 1850.

16. 'The Matron of the Workhouse Hospital', *The Galway Vindicator*, 14 December 1850.

17. 'Dirty Streets', *The Galway Vindicator*, 20 November 1850.

18. 'The Matron of the Workhouse Hospital'.

19. 'Galway Union: State of the House', *The Galway Vindicator*, 15 May 1850.

20. 'The Appeal of the Irish Poor', *The Galway Mercury*, 25 January 1847.

11 BACKLASH AND REBELLION

1. 'Midnight Legislation: Class Struggle in Ireland 1760–1840', available online at http://libcom.org/history/midnight-legislation-class-struggle-ireland-1760–1840 (accessed May 2009).

2. Henry, *St Clerans*, pp. 12, 19.

3. 'Conflict Between Police and Whiteboys', *The Galway Vindicator*, 9 May 1847.

4. 'Capture of Four Whiteboys', *The Galway Vindicator*, 28 February 1849.

5. 'Scarcity and Food Riots on the Continent', *The Galway Vindicator*, 22 May 1847.

6. 'Food Riots in the West of England', *The Galway Vindicator*, 22 May 1847.

7. Ó Cathaoir, *Famine Diary*, p. 51.

8. *Ibid.*, pp. 150–1.

9. 'Midnight Legislation: Class Struggle in Ireland 1760–1840'.

10. Ó Cathaoir, *Famine Diary*, p. 172.

11. Britannica Concise Encyclopedia, 'William Smith O'Brien', http://www.answers.com/topic/william-smith-o-brien (accessed May 2009).

12. A. H. Crealey, *An Irish Almanac: Notable Events in Ireland from 1014 to the Present*, Cork: Mercier Press, 1993, p. 101.

13. Britannica Concise Encyclopedia, 'William Smith O'Brien'.

14. 'Meagher, Thomas Francis', available online at http://www.infoplease.

com/ce6/people/A0832412.html (accessed May 2009).

15. J. Mitchell, 'Fr Peter Daly (*c.* 1788–1868)', *Journal of the Galway Archaeological and Historical Society*, 39 (1983–4), p. 58.

16. 'Courage Brothers', *The Galway Vindicator*, 14 June 1848.

12 ESCAPE FROM FAMINE

1. Henry, *Coffin Ship*, pp. 52–8.

2. Ó Cathaoir, *Famine Diary*, pp. 131–2.

3. 'Emigration: Deaths', *The Galway Vindicator*, 24 July 1847.

4. 'Irish Emigrants Refused Admission into Boston', *The Galway Vindicator*, 30 June 1847.

5. Ó Cathaoir, *Famine Diary*, p. 126.

6. 'Emigration', *The Galway Mercury*, 1 May 1847.

7. 'Free Emigration to New South Wales and Cape of Good Hope', *The Galway Vindicator*, 8 September 1847.

8. Henry, *Coffin Ship*, pp. 60–2.

9. 'Ill Treatment of Emigrants in Passenger Ships', *The Galway Vindicator*, 4 January 1851.

10. 'Most Cruel Inhumanity at Sea: Is It Murder?' *The Galway Vindicator*, 29 September 1849.

11. 'An Emigrant's Farewell', *The Galway Vindicator*, 3 July 1850.

13 VOYAGE OF HOPE AND DISASTER

1. 'To the Emigrants of 1849', *The Galway Vindicator*, 10 March 1849.

2. 'Hints to Emigrants to the United States', *The Galway Vindicator*, 23 September 1848.

3. 'Emigration', *The Galway Vindicator*, 7 April 1848.

4. 'The California Gold Region', *The Galway Vindicator*, 17 January 1849.

5. 'Halifax and Galway New Steam Line', *The Galway Vindicator*, 22 June 1850.

6. 'Good News for Ireland', *The Galway Vindicator*, 6 February 1850.
7. 'The Exile', *The Galway Vindicator*, 3 April 1849.
8. 'Emigration', *The Galway Vindicator*, 14 March 1849.
9. Henry, *Coffin Ship*, pp. 92–6.
10. *Ibid.*, pp. 98–100.
11. *Ibid.*, pp. 103–6.
12. *Ibid.*, pp. 106–9.
13. *Ibid.*, pp. 110–11.
14. 'Rhymes for the People', *The Galway Vindicator*, 6 March 1847.

14 EMIGRANT SOLDIERS

1. Henry, *Coffin Ship*, pp. 182–4.
2. Fogarty, J., 'The St. Patricio Battalion: The Irish Soldiers of Mexico', available online at http://www.irlandeses.org/sanpatriciosB.htm (accessed May 2009).
3. The Galway Association of New York, 'Colonel Patrick Kelly', *Galway Roots/Clanna na Gaillimhe*, 5 (1996), pp. 119–20.
4. A Briere & H. Hunt, *Hallowed Ground: Battlefields of the Civil War*, New York: Crescent Books, 1990, pp. 85–86, 112.
5. M. Dungan, *Distant Drums: Irish Soldiers in Foreign Armies*, Belfast: The Appletree Press Ltd, 1993, p. 31.
6. The Galway Association of New York, 'Colonel Patrick Kelly', p. 119.
7. Dungan, *Distant Drums*, p. 34.
8. Briere & Hunt, *Hallowed Ground*, p. 112.
9. The Galway Association of New York, 'Colonel Patrick Kelly', p. 119.
10. J. McCormack, 'Richard "Dick" Dowling: Battle of the Sabine McCormack Pass', lecture, 2000.
11. 'The Rebel Boy', *The Galway Vindicator*, 17 April 1850.

15 THE SILENT PEOPLE

1. Ó Cathaoir, *Famine Diary*, p. 161.

2. Walker, *One Man's Famine*, p. 101.
3. Ó Cathaoir, *Famine Diary*, p. 168.
4. 'Fatal Outrage at Patrington', *The Galway Vindicator*, 7 August 1850.
5. 'The Workhouse', *Galway Advertiser*, 3 March 1994.
6. Henry, *Coffin Ship*, pp. 182–5.
7. Kay, J. H., 'Hunger for Memorials: New York's Monument to the Irish Famine', available online at http://www.janeholtzkay.com/Articles/hunger.html (accessed May 2009).
8. 'Rhode Island Irish Famine Memorial Committee Inc.', available online at http://www.rifaminememorial.com (accessed May 2009).
9. Board of Directors, Ireland Park Foundation, 'The Making of Ireland Park, Toronto', available online at http://www.irelandparkfoundation.com/index.php (accessed May 2009).
10. Power, T., Irish Famine Commemoration Committee, 'Céad Míle Fáilte', available online at http://www.irishfaminememorial.org/default.htm (accessed May 2009).
11. Skibbereen Information Leaflet, May 2009.
12. 'Was This Murder?', *Galway Independent*, 23 September 2009.
13. 'God Help the Poor!', *The Galway Mercury*, 21 August 1847.

16   FAR-REACHING EFFECTS

1. 'All That Is Left: Scene at a Mayo Eviction', *The Illustrated London News*, 17 April 1886.
2. W. Henry, *Supreme Sacrifice: The Story of Éamonn Ceannt, 1881–1916*, Cork: Mercier Press, 2005, p. 3.
3. 'Absenteeism', *The Galway Mercury*, 27 March 1847.
4. D. Roche and M. Shiel, *A Forgotten Campaign and Aspects of the Heritage of South-East Galway*, Galway: East Galway Centenary Committee and Woodford Heritage Group, 1986, pp. 19–27.
5. 'The Exile', *The Galway Vindicator*, 3 April 1850.
6. Henry, *Supreme Sacrifice*, p. 28.
7. Ó Cathaoir, *Famine Diary*, p. 164.

8. J. Carty, *Ireland from the Great Famine to the Treaty of 1921: A Documentary Record*, Dublin: C. J. Fallon Ltd, 1966, p. 12.

9. B. Webb, 'Eva of *The Nation*: Poet and Patriot', *Galway Roots/Clanna na Gaillimhe*, 3 (1998), pp. 128–32.

10. C. Preston, *A School History of Ireland: Part II, 1607–1949*, Dublin: Browne and Nolan Ltd, no date, pp. 107–9.

11. Webb, 'Eva of *The Nation*: Poet and Patriot', pp. 131–2.

12. 'Eva of *The Nation*: Part 4', *Galway Independent*, 5 May 2010.

13. J. Cassidy, *Buses, Trains and Gaelic Games: A History of CIE GAA Clubs*, Dublin: Original Writing, 2009, pp. 1–4.

14. Henry, *Supreme Sacrifice*, p. 12.

15. K. O'Ceirin and C. O'Ceirin, *Women of Ireland: A Biographic Dictionary*, Galway: Tir Eolas, 1996, pp. 94–5.

16. The History Place, 'After the Famine', http://historyplace.com/worldhistory/famine/after.htm (April 2009).

17. Henry, *Supreme Sacrifice*, pp. 22, 59, 137–8.

18. Ó Cathaoir, *Famine Diary*, p. 167.

19. 'A Cry from the Land', *The Galway Vindicator*, 11 April 1849.

References

DOCUMENTS

Skibbereen Information Leaflet, May 2009

INTERNET PAGES (ACCESSED MAY 2009)

Anon., 'Meagher, Thomas Francis', available online at http://www.infoplease.com/ce6/people/A0832412.html

Anon., 'Midnight Legislation: Class Struggle in Ireland 1760–1840', available online at http://libcom.org/history/midnight-legislation-class-struggle-ireland-1760–1840

Anon., 'Randolph Routh + 1858', available online at http://genealogy.links.org/linkscgi/readged?/home/ben/camilla-genealogy/current+c-routh88898+2–2-0-1-0

Anon., 'Rhode Island Irish Famine Memorial Committee Inc.', available online at http://www.rifaminememorial.com

Board of Directors, Ireland Park Foundation, 'The Making of Ireland Park, Toronto', available online at http://www.irelandparkfoundation.com/index.php

Britannica Concise Encyclopedia, 'William Smith O'Brien', http://www.answers.com/topic/william-smith-o-brien

Fogarty, J., 'The St. Patricio Battalion: The Irish Soldiers of Mexico', available online at http://www.irlandeses.org/sanpatriciosB.htm12

The History Place, 'After the Famine', available online at historyplace.com/worldhistory/famine/after.htm

Kay, J. H., 'Hunger for Memorials: New York's Monument to the Irish Famine', available online at http://www.janeholtzkay.com/Articles/hunger.html

Oxford Companion to Irish History, 'Gregory Clause', available online at http://www.encyclopedia.com/doc/1O245-Gregoryclause.html

Power, T., Irish Famine Commemoration Committee, 'Céad Míle Fáilte', available online at http://www.irishfaminememorial.org/default.htm

The Reformation Online, 'The Great Irish Famine (1846–52), available online at http://www.reformation.org/irish_famine.html

JOURNALS

Galway Reader

McGuire, S., 'Famine Relief', 1950, vols 1 and 2, no. 3, pp. 71–2

——, 'Education: Galway Grammar School', 1950, vol. 3, nos 1 and 2, p. 56

Journal of the Galway Archaeological and Historical Society

Kerrigan, C., 'Temperance and Politics in Pre-Famine Galway', 1991, vol. 43, pp. 87, 89

Langan-Egan, M., 'Some Aspects of the Great Famine in Galway', 1999, vol. 51, pp. 122–32

Mitchell, J., 'Fr Peter Daly (*c.* 1788–1868)', 1983–4, vol. 39, p. 58

Galway Roots/Clanna na Gaillimhe, Journal of the Galway Family History Society

The Galway Association of New York, 'Colonel Patrick Kelly', 1996, vol. 5, p. 119

Murray, J. P., 'The Great Famine in Galway', 1996, vol. 3, pp. 1–3

Ó Laoi, P., 'The Famine in Castlegar', 1996, vol. 3, pp. 17–19

——, '1847: Famine in Galway ', 1996, vol. 3, pp. 59–60

Villiers-Tuthill, K., 'The Clifden Union', 1996, vol. 3, pp. 6–7

Webb, B., 'Eva of *The Nation*: Poet and Patriot', 1998, vol. 3, pp. 128–132

LECTURE

McCormack, J., 'Richard "Dick" Dowling: Battle of the Sabine McCormack Pass', lecture delivered to the Galway Archaeological and Historical Society, GMIT, Galway, May 2000

MAGAZINES

'All That Is Left: Scene at a Mayo Eviction', *The Illustrated London News*, 17 April 1886

O'Dowd, P., 'The Famine: Think About It!', *St Patrick's Parish Christmas Magazine*, Galway, 1995, pp. 21–2

'Sketches of Ireland', *The Illustrated London News*, 16 July 1870

NEWSPAPERS

Galway Advertiser

'An Unseemly Brawl over God and Scripture', 13 November 2008

'Nuns' Island Whiskey', 6 August 2009

'Steaming Along', 14 May 1992

'The Workhouse', 3 March 1994

Galway Independent

'Eva of *The Nation*: Part 4', 5 May 1010

'The Great Famine's Effect on Galway', 29 July 2009

'Was This Murder?', 23 September 2009

The Galway Mercury

'Absenteeism', 27 March 1847

'The Appeal of the Irish Poor', 25 January 1847

'Claddagh Relief Establishment', 30 January 1847

'The Commissariat', 13 May 1848

'The Devon Commission', 26 June 1847

'Distress in the West', 13 June 1847

'Emigration', 1 May 1847

'Extermination in the County', 17 June 1848

'Extermination: The Court of Chancery', 30 October 1847

'A Famine Report', 13 March 1847

'The Famine Stricken', 13 February 1847

'Galway Union: State of the House', 24 March 1849

'God Help the Poor!', 21 August 1847

'Gregory's Quarter Acre', 27 January 1849

'The Irish Labourers' *Pater Nostre*', 16 January 1847

'Irish Sufferings: Whig and Tory Sympathy', 3 July 1847

'Just Found Out: Horrible Oh! Horrible', 18 March 1848

'Lament of the Ejected Irish Peasant', 12 January 1850

'A Lay of Sorrow', 20 February 1847

'More Deaths by Starvation', 23 January 1847

'More Deaths by Starvation', 22 January 1848

'Mortality Amongst the Gentry', 1 May 1847

'Murder in Costello', 10 October 1847

'Notice', 24 January 1846

'Notice to Paupers Receiving Outdoor Relief', 22 January 1848

'Orphan's Breakfast Institute', 31 July 1847

'The Poor Man's Christmas: A Carol for the Year of Famine', 2 January 1847

'The Potato Crop', 25 October 1845

'Spread of Fever', 20 May 1847

'Starvation', 16 January 1847

'State of the Town', 29 January 1848

'Unsound Food', 29 July 1848

'Widows and Orphans Asylum', 22 January 1848

The Galway Vindicator

'Additional Poor House', 9 February 1848

'American Relief for Galway', 21 July 1847

'Another Victim Among the Clergy: Death of the Rev. J. Roche RCC', 4
 September 1847

'Assistant Chaplain to the Workhouse', 27 November 1847

'Awful Mortality in the Ballinasloe Workhouses', 12 May 1849

'The California Gold Region', 17 January 1849

'Capture of Four Whiteboys', 28 February 1849

'Claddagh Curing House', 13 January 1849

'A Claddagh Fisherman', 24 March 1849

'Claddagh Piscatory School', 29 September 1847

'Come to the Rescue', 10 April 1847

'Committals to Our County Prison: State of the Country', 17 July 1850

'Conflict Between Police and Whiteboys', 9 May 1847

'Courage Brothers', 14 June 1848

'A Cry from the Land', 11 April 1849

'The Curse of the Whigs', 17 April 1847

'Death of Major M'Kie', 20 June 1849

'Death of Marcus Lynch', 29 January 1848

'Death of the Admiral of the Claddagh Fishermen', 28 April 1849

'Deaths from Starvation', 14 February 1849

'Decrease of the Population', 31 October 1849

'Deep Sea Fishery', 11 July 1849

'Destitution in Galway', 10 February 1849

'Dirty Streets', 20 November 1850

'An Emigrant's Farewell', 3 July 1850

'Emigration', 7 April 1848

'Emigration', 14 March 1849

'Emigration: Deaths', 24 July 1847

'Evictions of Householders in Galway', 30 January 1850

'The Exile', 3 April 1850

'Extermination', 23 September 1848

'Fatal Outrage at Patrington', 7 August 1850

'Fever in Galway', 23 October 1847

'A Few Days', 27 January 1849

'Food Riots', 6 October 1847

'Food Riots in the West of England', 22 May 1847

'Free Emigration to New South Wales and Cape of Good Hope', 8 September 1847

'Frightful Destitution in Mayo', 17 February 1849

'Frightful Influx of Evicted Cottier Paupers', 18 December 1847

'Galway Herring Fishery', 24 August 1850

'Galway Industrial Society', 23 June 1847

'Galway Union: State of the House', 15 May 1850

'Good News for Ireland', 6 February 1850

'Halifax and Galway New Steam Line', 22 June 1850

'Herring Fishery', 15 September 1847

'Hints to Emigrants to the United States', 23 September 1848

'Ill Treatment of Emigrants in Passenger Ships', 4 January 1851

'Irish Emigrants Refused Admission into Boston', 30 June 1847

'Irish Extermination', 8 April 1848

'The Irish Fisheries', 2 October 1849

'The Matron of the Workhouse Hospital', 14 December 1850

'Miserable Conditions of the Poor in Galway', 1 December 1848

'Most Cruel Inhumanity at Sea: Is It Murder?', 29 September 1849

'More Evictions', 5 July 1848

'Outrage', 18 December 1847

'The Poor Man's Harvest: A Dirge', 13 October 1847

'The Process of Slow Poisoning: Diet of the "Mere Irish" Pauper', 12 May 1849

'The Rebel Boy', 17 April 1850

'Rhymes for the People', 6 March 1847

'Scarcity and Food Riots on the Continent', 22 May 1847

'The Society of Friends', 20 October 1847

'Starvation: Inquest', 13 March 1847

'State of the County and Town Prison', 10 February 1849

'State of the People', 31 March 1847

'State of the Town and of the Prisons', 28 February 1849

'To the Emigrants of 1849', 10 March 1849
'Town Commissioners', 4 September 1847
'Two Deaths from the effects of Starvation', 28 February 1849
'Want of Burial Ground', 2 June 1847
'We Are Starving, Bread or Employment', 8 May 1847
'The Working of the Poor Law', 10 March 1849

The Tablet
'Letter to the Editor', 23 May 1848

BIBLIOGRAPHY

Bicentenary Committee, *By The Narrow Gate: A Bicentenary History*, Galway: Bicentenary Committee, 2008

Briere, A. & Hunt, H., *Hallowed Ground; Battlefields of the Civil War*, New York: Crescent Books, New York, 1990

Carty, J., *Ireland from the Great Famine to the Treaty of 1921: A Documentary Record*, Dublin: C. J. Fallon Ltd, 1966

Casserly, J., *An Open Door: A History of the St Vincent de Paul Society, 1849–1999*, Galway: St Vincent de Paul Society, 1999

Cassidy, J., *Buses, Trains and Gaelic Games: A History of CIE GAA Clubs*, Dublin: Original Writing Ltd, 2009

Crealey, A. H., *An Irish Almanac: Notable Events in Ireland from 1014 to the Present*, Cork: Mercier Press, 1993

Dungan, M., *Distant Drums: Irish Soldiers in Foreign Armies*, Belfast: The Appletree Press Ltd, 1993

Garvey, G., *Bushypark Celebrates, 1837–1987*, Galway: Fr Gerard Garvey, 1988

Henry, W., *St Clerans: The Tale of a Manor House*, Galway: Merv Griffin, 1999

—— *Role of Honour: Mayors of Galway City, 1485–2001*, Galway: Galway City Council, 2001

—— *Supreme Sacrifice: The Story of Éamonn Ceannt, 1881–1916*, Cork: Mercier Press, 2005

—— *Coffin Ship: The Wreck of the Brig St John*, Cork: Mercier Press, 2009

Litton, H., *The Irish Famine: An Illustrated History*, Dublin: Wolfhound Press, 1994

MacLochlainn, A. and Regan, T., *Two Galway Schools*, Galway: Galway Labour History Group, 1993

Ó Cathaoir, B., *Famine Diary*, Dublin: Irish Academic Press, 1999

O'Ceirin, K. and O'Ceirin, C., *Women of Ireland: A Biographic Dictionary*, Galway: Tir Eolas, 1996

O'Dowd, P., *Galway City Waterways: A Walking Tour*, Galway: Peadar O'Dowd, 1985

—— *Old and New Galway*, Galway: The Archaeological, Historical and Folklore Society, Regional Technical College, Galway, and The Connacht Tribune Ltd, 1985

—— *Down by the Claddagh*, Galway: Kenny's Bookshop and Art Galleries Ltd, 1993

—— *The Great Famine and the West, 1845–1850*, Galway: Galway City Council, 1995

Preston, C., *A School History of Ireland: Part II, 1607–1949*, Dublin: Browne and Nolan Ltd, no date

Roche, D. and Shiel, M., *A Forgotten Campaign and Aspects of the Heritage of South-East Galway*, Galway: East Galway Centenary Committee and Woodford Heritage Group, 1986

Semple, M., *Reflections on Lough Corrib*, Galway: Maurice Semple, 1974

Walker, L. H., *One Man's Famine*, Galway: Centenary Committee, 1978

White, R., *1847 Famine Ship Diary*, Cork: Mercier Press, 1994

Woodham-Smith, C., *The Great Hunger*, New York: Harper & Row, 1991

Also available from Mercier Press

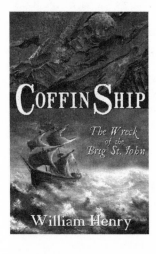

COFFIN SHIP: THE WRECK OF THE
BRIG *ST. JOHN*

William Henry

ISBN: 978 1 85635 631 2

The story of the Brig *St. John*, which
sailed for America loaded with
passengers desperate to escape the
ravages of the Great Famine, but
sank off the coast of Massachusetts
in October 1849.

FORGOTTEN HEROES:
GALWAY SOLDIERS OF THE GREAT
WAR 1914–1918

William Henry

ISBN: 978 1 85635 556 8

A meticulously researched record of
Galwaymen who fought and died in
the Great War.

www.mercierpress.ie

Also available from Mercier Press

ROBERT WHYTE'S 1847 FAMINE SHIP DIARY

ISBN: 978 1 85635 091 4

The moving diary of one of the passengers on the *Ajax*, describing the trials and tribulations of the journey from Dublin to Canada for those escaping the Great Famine in Ireland.

THE GREAT IRISH FAMINE

Cathal Póirtéir (ed.)

ISBN: 978 1 85635 111 9

This wide-ranging series of essays looks at all aspects of the Great Famine, from the suffering brought about by the failure of the potato crop to the far-reaching effects that the famine had on Irish society, politics and agriculture.

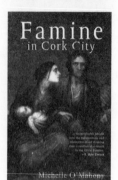

FAMINE IN CORK CITY

Michelle O'Mahony

ISBN: 978 1 85635 455 4

When the Great Famine struck in Ireland, thousands fled to the hated workhouses seeking relief from their suffering. *Famine in Cork City* explores life in the Cork Union Workhouse and sheds light on the horrific conditions endured by the inmates.

www.mercierpress.ie

MERCIER PRESS

IRISH PUBLISHER - IRISH STORY

We hope you enjoyed this book.

Since 1944, Mercier Press has published books that have been critically important to Irish life and culture. Books that dealt with subjects that informed readers about Irish scholars, Irish writers, Irish history and Ireland's rich heritage.

We believe in the importance of providing accessible histories and cultural books for all readers and all who are interested in Irish cultural life.

Our website is the best place to find out more information about Mercier, our books, authors, news and the best deals on a wide variety of books. Mercier tracks the best prices for our books online and we seek to offer the best value to our customers, offering free delivery within Ireland.

Sign up on our website or complete and return the form below to receive updates and special offers.

www.mercierpress.ie
www.facebook.com/mercier.press
www.twitter.com/irishpublisher

Name:
Email:
Address:
Mobile No.:

Mercier Press, Unit 3b, Oak House, Bessboro Rd, Blackrock, Cork, Ireland